100 EVENTS
THAT SHAPED WORLD HISTORY

BILL YENNE

Copyright © 1993, 2023 by Sourcebooks
Text by Bill Yenne
Cover design by Will Riley
Internal illustrations by Westchester Publishing Services
Cover and internal design © 2023 by Sourcebooks

Published by Sourcebooks eXplore, an imprint of Sourcebooks Kids
P.O. Box 4410, Naperville, Illinois 60567-4410
(630) 961-3900
sourcebookskids.com

Originally published in 1993 by Bluewood Books, a division of The Siyeh Group, Inc.

Cataloging-in-Publication Data is on file with the Library of Congress.

Source of Production: Versa Press, East Peoria, Illinois, USA
Date of Production: September 2023
Run Number: 5033353

Printed and bound in the United States of America.
VP 10 9 8 7 6 5 4 3 2 1

CONTENTS

1   2 3 4   5   6 7   8   9 10 11 12 13 14 15 16 17 18 19   20 21 22 23 24 25

Timeline of Events

20,000 BCE   **1066 CE**

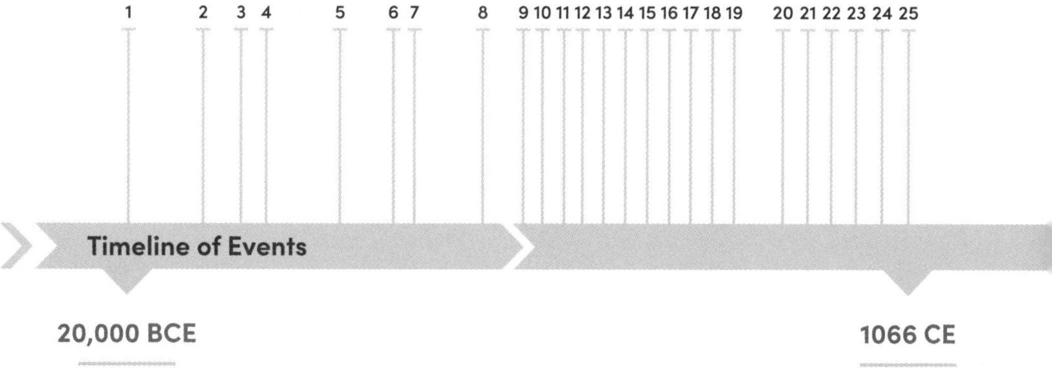

43

26 27 28   29 30 31 32 33   34 35   36 37 38   39 40 41 42 44 45 46 47 48 49 50 51 52 53

Timeline of Events

1096

1865

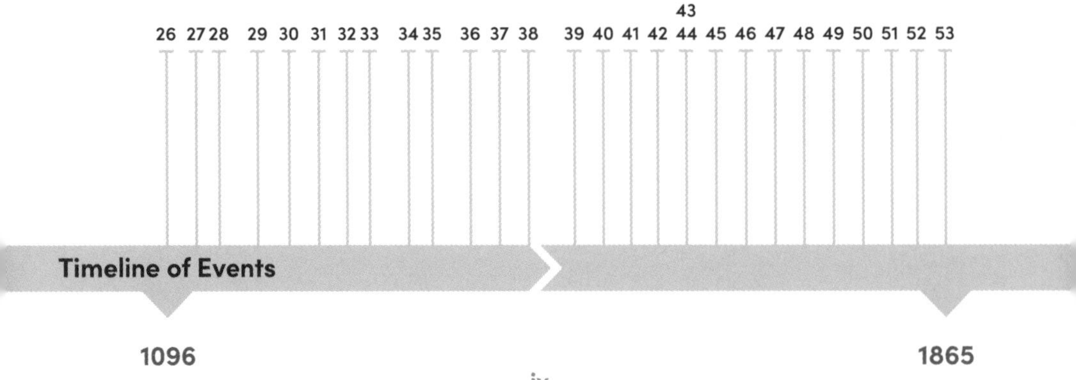

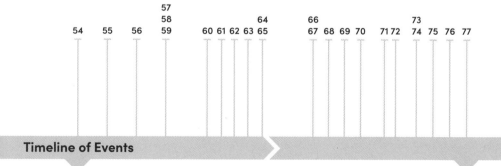

Timeline of Events

1868

1942

84
88
78 79 80 81 82 83 85 86 87 89 90 91 92 93 94 95 96 97 98 99 100

Timeline of Events

1942 2001

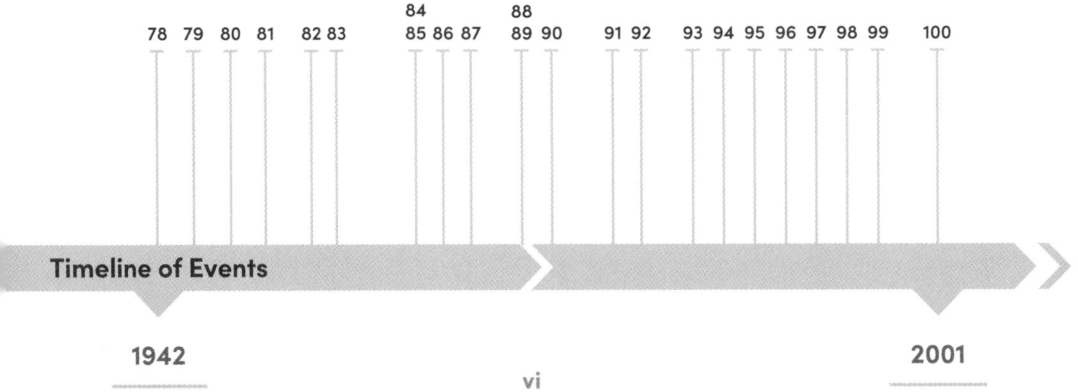

INTRODUCTION

THE HISTORY of our human civilization is like a highway our ancestors have traveled since the dawn of time. Like any highway, it is not a straight road, but one marked by twists and turns, by hills and valleys, and by milestones. The historical milestones are not freestanding pillars. They are more like dominoes. Later events often happen only because of earlier events. For instance, the Battles of Salamis and Plataea were significant because they prevented the annihilation of Greek civilization. This in turn allowed a great flourishing of Greek culture, which gave rise to the philosophies whose thought would form the basis for Western culture. The Battle of Waterloo and the World Wars changed the course of history. So did the invention of the steam engine and the airplane. Interplanetary flights have also cast a completely new perspective on our relatively tiny planet.

The events included in this book are many and varied, but they all have one thing in common: after they happened our conception of our world's place in the universe changed—permanently and dramatically.

If this book is Eurocentric, it is because the Western conception of history is linear rather than cyclical, as in the East, and it has been recorded that way—a highway of events marked by milestones. It is also because the Europeans—for better or worse—were the explorers and the catalysts of change. Marco Polo opened the door between Europe and China. Christopher Columbus made way between the Old World and the New World. If the Chinese opened trade routes into Europe, or the Sioux colonized England or Japan, our conception of history would have taken quite a different turn.

The intent of this book is to make history accessible and fun. Have a look at the timeline, which places these one hundred events in the context of time. Challenge yourself and your friends with the projects in the back of this book. It's fun to discuss and debate which events you might have included or deleted.

This book is a capsule view of some of history's most important milestones. Our goal has been to present these milestones in their historical context and to give our readers some basic information about how they came about: who made them happen and why they were important.

Petroglyphs

◆ **WHEN WAS** the dawn of **history**? It is hard, if not impossible, to pinpoint the moment when all those events that we call **prehistoric** gave way to those that are part of our history. It was not a moment at all, but a long, gradual process that developed over many, many years.

Human beings were on the earth a half million years ago. Bones discovered in the 1970s of the *Australopithecus afarensis*—the apelike creature that scientists believe to be the ancestor of modern humans—date back nearly four million years. There is also evidence that human beings were making tools and living in groups on all the continents 30,000 years ago. **Petroglyphs**, or rock paintings, have been found that date back to at least 10,000 years ago, and there are elaborate murals painted on the walls of caves in Spain and France dating back 18,000 years.

So, if humans have been on the earth for thousands of centuries, how and where did history begin? The dawn of history probably occurred independently in all parts of the world inhabited by people, beginning with a spoken language and, in turn, leading to stories. Storytellers would retell tales of events that had happened in the past. In this way, the myths and legends of the world's cultures were born.

Many early stories were lost, but some may have survived, gradually evolving into ancient legends that are still remembered today. The dawn of history was when legends were first passed from one generation to the next.

HUMAN BEINGS had first formed themselves into groups or bands by 20,000 BCE. These groups lived together in camps, which were often semipermanent. In the beginning, there were not any lasting settlements because people were nomadic. They moved with the seasons and followed their sources of food, which included wild animals and seasonal plants.

In the Middle East around 8000 BCE, people first discovered that they could control the plants and animals that provided their food. They learned to cultivate fields and gardens and to gather herds of sheep and cattle. Soon the area around the Tigris and Euphrates Rivers, in what is now Syria and Iraq, became known as the **Fertile Crescent**.

It was here, in ancient Mesopotamia (from the Greek words *meso*, meaning "between" and *potamia*, meaning "river") that large numbers of people ceased to be nomadic and started building concentrations of permanent dwellings. These were the first cities. By 6000 BCE, the Fertile Crescent had also become the **"Cradle of Civilization."** In these cities, people set up systems of government to rule themselves and the societies that developed because of them living together permanently.

Egyptian hieroglyphics

THE ABILITY to draw or write symbols with meanings is unique to the human species, and it is one of the most important differences between us and all other creatures. Humans were drawing and painting symbols on rocks more than 40,000 years ago, and such illustrations were an important part of people's lives for centuries.

However, it was not until about 3,200 BCE that people had the idea of developing a phonetic writing system—a set of simple, widely understood symbols that represented the sounds used in speech and could be combined in different ways to make words and sentences.

One of the earliest phonetic writing systems was **cuneiform**, a script developed by the ancient Sumerians. Its widespread use throughout the Mesopotamian region preceded Egyptian **hieroglyphics**. It was from cuneiform that the Hebrew and Arabic alphabets were derived. It was also a precursor of the Greek alphabet, which in turn led to the **Roman alphabet** used today in English, French, German, and most other western languages. The **Cyrillic alphabet** used in Russia and other Slavic countries also developed from the ancient Greek alphabet. The Chinese writing system was created later than those of the ancient Middle East and was used as the basis for the writing systems elsewhere in Asia, such as in Japan and Korea.

The pharaohs were responsible for many landmarks in Egypt, like the Sphinx and the Great Pyramid

world's first empire. Under the rule of the pharaohs, which lasted 2,500 years, Egypt became a culture unlike anything seen before.

Individual towns and cities no longer had to be self-sufficient, and they became interdependent. At the center of this society, the pharaoh's court developed great wealth and power—both political and religious. The pharaoh became more than a king; he was worshipped as a god. Great cities and huge engineering projects were undertaken. Between 3800 and 2500 BCE, for example, over thirty-five massive pyramids were built as tombs for the pharaohs. The Great Pyramid, erected under the rule of **Pharaoh Cheops (2700–2675 BCE)**, stands as tall as a forty-five story building.

The Egyptian pyramids and the other great structures are evidence of the most advanced culture of its time, but they are only part of the story. The centralization of the empire made possible the development of the arts and sciences—especially mathematics and astronomy—beyond the levels previously known anywhere else in the world.

THE FIRST cities that appeared in Mesopotamia's Fertile Crescent were **city-states**. They were self-sufficient and self-governing within their walls. Their influence extended only to the surrounding agricultural land owned and operated by the people in the city-state, plus whatever small, nearby villages that were dependent on the city. A monarch's rule usually extended no farther than he could see from a hill.

This pattern changed around 3300 BCE when the towns and villages along the Nile River formed into the two kingdoms of Upper and Lower Egypt. In 3100 BCE, the Egyptian pharaoh (king) **Menes** unified the two regions into a single entity, which constituted the

AS PEOPLE formed societies, there was a need for rules to regulate individuals' behavior for the benefit of the group. In the earliest cultures, there were a few rules, and those rules dealt with obvious transgressions, such as a violation of personal and property rights. As the city-states of Mesopotamia and the great kingdoms of Egypt formed, the rules became more complex. The rules were imposed by the kings to control the people in order to benefit the monarchy and the realm.

During the reign of the Babylonian king **Hammurabi (1792–1750 BCE)**, the first true legal code was issued. A well-known and well-respected monarch, Hammurabi is remembered for putting "the rule of righteousness in the land." Discovered in the ruins of ancient Babylon in 1901 by French archaeologists led by Jacques de Morgan, the **Code of Hammurabi** was carved in cuneiform characters on a huge stone slab. There were 282 laws in the Code, with evidence of another thirty-five having been chipped off and lost.

The Code identified specific crimes and stipulated specific penalties. For instance, a man who failed to repair his floodwall would be compelled to compensate a neighbor whose land was flooded. A priestess could be burned alive for entering a tavern without permission. A widow could inherit an equal portion of her husband's property that their son inherited. And a surgeon whose patient died while under the knife would lose his hand. The Code also allowed a debtor a way out by giving his wife or child to a creditor for three years.

The Code went beyond being simply a legal code. It stipulated the structure of the government. And, since the king was also the chief priest, the Code governed Babylonian religious life as well.

The stone slab that the Code of Hammurabi was carved into

The Code of Hammurabi was a milestone of world history. For the first time, laws were published and codified for all to see rather than enacted by the monarch's whim. In this sense, the Code was a precursor of the legal systems under which most modern societies function.

MOST ANCIENT religions—such as those in Mesopotamia, Egypt, India, Greece, and later Rome—were **polytheistic**, meaning that their followers believed in many gods and goddesses, such as a god of the sun, a goddess of the moon, and so on. However, one particular group was **monotheistic**, believing in a single deity whom they called **Jehovah**. These people were the Hebrews, the twelve tribes of Israel, and their religion was **Judaism**. In the beginning, monotheism was a distinctly minority belief, but today, it is the central doctrine for over half of the world's religiously faithful. This is due to the words preserved in the Jewish scriptures, particularly the **Torah**, which is essentially the same document as the Christian **Old Testament**.

There are many important events in the history of the Jewish people, but the event which has had the most far-reaching impact on Jewish and Christian doctrine occurred when the prophet **Moses (1400–1270? BCE)** received the Ten Commandments on Mount Sinai.

The Hebrews were defeated by the Egyptians and taken to Egypt as slaves. At one point, an edict was issued calling for all Hebrew boys to be killed. Moses was saved from this fate when his mother put him in a basket made of reeds and set him adrift on the Nile River. He was discovered by the pharaoh's daughter and cared for in the palace. When he grew to manhood, he lobbied for the emancipation of his people, which **King Ramses II (1292–1225 BCE)** reluctantly granted. Moses led the Hebrew people out of Egypt, whereupon they are said to have spent forty years wandering in the Sinai Desert en route to their homeland in Israel. It was about 1250 BCE that—according to Biblical scripture—God appeared to Moses on the upper slopes of Mount Sinai, and he gave Moses two stone tablets containing a set of laws known as the **Ten Commandments**. Moses took these back to his people, and they adopted them as the basic moral code of Judaism. Christianity subsequently embraced the Ten Commandments, and today, they are among the basic beliefs of over two billion people.

THE TEN COMMANDMENTS

1. *I am the Lord, your God, who brought you out of the land of Egypt, that place of slavery. You shall have no other gods before me.*

2. *You shall not carve idols for yourselves in the shape of anything in the sky above or on the earth below or in the waters beneath the sea. You shall not bow down before them or worship them.*

3. *You shall not take the name of the Lord, your God, in vain.*

4. *Remember to keep holy the Sabbath day. Six days you may labor and do all your work, but the seventh day is the Sabbath of the Lord, your God, and no work may be done by you. In six days the Lord made the heavens and the earth, the seas and all that is in them, but on the seventh day he rested. That is why the Lord has blessed the Sabbath day and made it holy.*

5. *Honor your father and your mother, that you may have a long life in the land, which the Lord, your God, has given you.*

6. *You shall not kill.*

7. *You shall not commit adultery.*

8. *You shalt not steal.*

9. *You shall not bear false witness against your neighbor.*

10. *You shall not covet your neighbor's house. You shall not covet your neighbor's wife, nor anything else that belongs to him.*

EARLY HUMAN civilizations had little contact with cultures other than those geographically adjacent. This continued even after the rise of the great civilizations in Egypt and Mesopotamia. The Egyptians had contact with the Nubians to the south and the Mesopotamians to the east, whereas the Mesopotamians interacted with the Persians and the other cultures to their north and east. Although some hearty souls certainly traveled well beyond the political orbit, there seems to have been little interest in empire building or even trade beyond closely defined influential spheres.

This changed with the **Phoenicians**, a people who lived on the far eastern shore of the Mediterranean Sea, which is now Lebanon. Facing the sea with their backs to the mountains, the Phoenicians were a seafaring people. They became the world's first major maritime trading power, extending their commercial ties beyond the ends of the earth and they remained the only such power for centuries. The Phoenicians were also the first people in the ancient Middle East to develop sustained contact with Europe. As such, their voyages became a turning point in world history.

The Phoenician fleet, which included military and commercial vessels, visited practically every port on both sides of the Mediterranean. The fleet sailed beyond the Straits of Gibraltar into the Atlantic Ocean and called at ports in northern Europe and down the coast of Africa. Some people have suggested that they reached the coast of North America. The Phoenicians also colonized lands from Cyprus to Corsica to Spain, and in 814 BCE they founded **Carthage** (in present-day Tunisia), which was destined to become one of the most powerful city-states in the Mediterranean region.

The Phoenicians were the first in the ancient Middle East to develop sustained contact with Europe

More than just merchants, the Phoenicians also invented and developed glassblowing. They were the first people to make wares of transparent and translucent glass on a mass scale, which became an important element in their trade.

THE ROMAN EMPIRE is perhaps the most significant political entity in Western history prior to the nineteenth century. The empire included most of Western Europe, from present-day England to Gibraltar and from the Rhineland to the Black Sea, Turkey, and all of North Africa, from the Mediterranean Sea to the edges of the Sahara Desert. Every shore Mediterranean waters touched was Roman territory.

Roman political organization, Roman literature, and the Roman alphabet greatly influenced the succeeding cultures of Europe and the Americas. Yet, before there was a Roman Empire, there was Rome, a city on the western side of the Italian peninsula. Legend has long held that Rome was founded in 753 BCE, which is now confirmed by archaeological evidence.

According to legend, there were two brothers, Amulius and Numitor, who was the king of **Alba Longa** (now central Italy). Amulius killed his brother and his brother's sons and claimed the throne. This plan succeeded until Numitor's daughter, Rhea Silvia, had twin sons. Amulius ordered her jailed and the twins thrown into the Tiber River. They survived and washed ashore at the foot of the Palatine Hill, where a she-wolf nursed them. Faustulus, a herdsman, found the boys, and he and his wife named them **Romulus** and **Remus**. In 753 BCE, the two brothers founded a new city on the Palatine Hill, located in modern Rome. However, they had many quarrels, which ultimately led to Romulus killing his brother.

The city, named Rome after Romulus, grew in importance, and Romulus undertook a policy of empire building that involved annexing adjacent lands by coercion and conquest. This was the beginning of an empire that would last a thousand years.

According to legend, Romulus and Remus were nursed by a she-wolf

TWO OF the five great organized world religions with the largest number of adherents—**Judaism** and **Hinduism**—trace their roots to antiquity and have no specific founder; however, rabbis teach that Judaism began when the Hebrew patriarch, **Abraham**, obeyed God. The other three world religions—**Buddhism**, **Christianity**, and Islam—were established in historical times by specific persons.

Buddhism began in northern India by a man named **Siddhartha Gautama**, who was born in 563 BCE to a wealthy family associated with the **Kshatriya**, the warrior aristocracy. He developed an early interest in philosophy and the literature of the **Vedas**, the basic scriptures of Hinduism. Gradually, however, he became disenchanted with Hinduism and the suffering that he saw around him and decided to develop an alternate religious philosophy that promised to deliver the spirit, if not the body, from earthly afflictions.

At age twenty-nine, Siddhartha snuck out of his palace for the first time. While he was out, he encountered an old man, a person suffering from disease, a dead body, and a very strictly religious man. These sights convinced him to abandon his palace as well as his wife and son, renounce all worldly possessions, and set out in search of the "truth." He visited many holy men and spent several years fasting and meditating. His objective was to find a way to overcome all bodily desires—including hunger—and to gain complete control over his mind. The truth that he sought eluded him until one night in May of 528 BCE, when, while sitting under a Bo Tree, he received what is known to Buddhists as **enlightenment**. In this single moment, Siddhartha realized that suffering could be conquered.

One of the basic doctrines of Hinduism is the cycle of **reincarnation**. The soul of every living thing that dies is reborn in another living thing. This cycle continues, with the

Siddhartha Gautama took the name "Buddha," meaning "Enlightened One"

soul gradually moving up from an insect to an animal to a human. If humans are evil in their lifetime, they will be reborn as a lower form of life; otherwise, they are reborn as another person. This cycle of reincarnation is infinite, but Siddhartha's enlightenment involved his realization that by following the proper path—Dharma—of meditation and devotion, the soul could achieve a state of Nirvana, a perfect final state not unlike the Judeo-Christian concept of heaven.

Siddhartha took the name **Buddha**, meaning **Enlightened One**, and went out into the world to teach his philosophy. After his death in 483 BCE, his followers founded orders of monks, and the Buddhist philosophy spread throughout Asia, finding a greater proportion of adherents in China, Japan, and Southeast Asia than in India. Today, there are over 500 million Buddhists in the world.

IN THE fifth century BCE, when Egypt's era as a mighty imperial power was a distant memory, and the tranquil days of the Roman Empire were still far in the future, two superpowers emerged in the world, each one representing a culture unlike the other. On one side there was Greece, whose philosophy and literature would form the kernel of European civilization,

and on the other was the Persian Empire (also called the Achaemenid Empire), a civilization that molded the culture and identity of the Middle East and other parts of Asia.

Cyrus the Great (c. 590–c. 529 BCE) founded the Persian Empire by uniting the tribes of Persia and extending the boundaries of his domain from the Mediterranean Sea to the Indus River in India. His grandson, **Darius (550–486 BCE)**, who ascended the throne in 522 BCE, consolidated Persian rule over Egypt and added the Phoenician fleet to his forces. His next goal was to conquer Greece and to extend the Persian Empire into Europe.

Darius had hoped to play on the internal disagreements among the Greek city-states, but they were able to set aside their differences and unite their forces to turn back his armies. Though outnumbered by the Persians, the better-trained Greeks defeated them at the **Battle of Marathon** in 490 BCE.

Ten years later, Darius's son, **Xerxes (519–465 BCE)**, gathered an even larger army. Supported by naval units, the Persian forces marched on Greece with an estimated 360,000 troops. The first major victory of the campaign went to the Greeks on September 23, 480 BCE, when the Greeks lured the Persian fleet into the narrow straits off the island of **Salamis**, outmaneuvered the ships, and destroyed them. Xerxes regrouped over the winter, returned the following year, and met the Greeks in battle on the **Plain of Plataea**. Again, as had been the case at Marathon and Salamis, an outnumbered Greek force succeeded in overtaking and defeating the larger and more powerful Persian army.

Xerxes's defeat at Plataea marked the beginning of the end of the Persian Empire. No longer expanding, it began to collapse from within, and by the end of the next century, it was ripe for conquest by Greek armies under **Alexander the Great (345–323 BCE)**.

Although no one could imagine it at the time, the Battle of Plataea would prove to be one of the most important turning points in world history. Had Darius or Xerxes prevailed, Greece would have fallen under Persian influence. As a conquered culture, the great flourishing of Greek science and literature that came in the last half of the fifth century would probably never have happened, and the profound impact of Greek civilization on Roman, and later European, cultures would never have occurred.

It was on one long summer day in 479 BCE that the course—and very essence—of European history was cast.

AS WE noted in our introduction, the milestones of history are like dominoes. Earlier events cause later events. The Battles of Salamis and Plataea were significant because they prevented the annihilation of Greek civilization. This, in turn, allowed a great flourishing of Greek culture, which gave rise to the philosophers who were largely responsible for formulating the basis of modern Western culture.

Throughout history, and in many cultures, there have been numerous outstanding thinkers, writers, and theoreticians, but in Athens during this period, there was a larger concentration of great minds—and they exerted a more profound impact on Western history—than the world would see in a small space and time until the Renaissance.

Among these are three whose names stand out above the others. **Socrates (c. 470–399 BCE)** was the first, and he was the teacher of **Plato (427–347 BCE)**. Plato, in turn, taught **Aristotle (384–322 BCE)**. This creative continuity added significantly to the depth and fullness of the birth of Western philosophical thought.

Socrates, who developed a following because of his witty oration, was also a brilliant philosopher who many consider the father of Western philosophy. Socrates believed humans existed for a purpose and right and wrong played a crucial role in defining our relationship with the environment and other people. He theorized that the purpose of an ideal government embodied wise men ruling for the good of society.

Plato embraced Socrates's ideas and elaborated on them in his book *The Republic*, wherein he discussed justice and how it should function in a perfect society. He advocated the pursuit of wisdom rather than the acceptance of dogma.

Greek philosophers Plato and Aristotle

Aristotle studied medicine as well as philosophy and applied a systematic method to the study of the human relationship with other aspects of the world around us. Aristotle was Alexander the Great's tutor. Aristotelian thought was ultimately harmonized with Christian theology by **St. Thomas Aquinas (1225–1274)** in the thirteenth century.

◆ **AS MODERN** western philosophy was built upon the foundations laid by Socrates, Plato, and Aristotle, modern medicine can also trace its roots to the golden age of Greek civilization. **Hippocrates (460–377 BCE)**, a Greek physician, originated the concept that in curing the sick, a doctor should "consider the nature of humans in general, and of each individual and the characteristics of each disease." In other words, a doctor should consider the interrelationship within the entire human mechanism rather than simply focusing on specific symptoms.

At the time, most of the world's medical problems were treated through ineffective means like rituals, magic, and prayer. However, Hippocrates, who had a much more progressive understanding of healing, wrote texts on medicine and medical ethics. In his writing, he advanced ideas that were centuries ahead of his time.

Hippocrates recognized that it was important for broken bones to be aligned in order to heal them properly. Traction had to be applied to both ends of a fracture, and then gradually released as the parts fitted together. He also encouraged a holistic approach, urging doctors to look beyond the local fracture to the patient's total reaction. Mobilization was recommended at an early stage, since "exercise strengthens and inactivity wastes." Today, this maxim is still followed in the doctor's attempt to avoid "atrophy of disuse."

Scientifically, Hippocrates's work was fairly limited. His ideas about blood circulation, for example, were simply wrong. However, while he left most scientific discoveries for later generations, he did formulate the theoretical base and the methods and procedures by which medicine would evolve over the coming centuries. Indeed, Hippocrates literally constructed

Hippocrates

the framework of modern medical practice. The **Hippocratic Oath**, which he wrote, is still the cornerstone of modern medical ethics. Included within the Hippocratic Oath are such basic tenets as doctor–patient confidentiality, a doctor's responsibilities regarding his patients, and a doctor's duty to treat anyone, regardless of their societal status.

◆ **WHAT THE** Persians failed to do in the fifth century BCE, a Greek general succeeded in doing in the fourth century BCE: establish a vast empire that straddled both Europe and Asia and stretched from Greece to India. The man's name was Alexander. We know him as **Alexander the Great (356–323 BCE)**.

Alexander's father, **Philip II of Macedonia**, brought all of Greece under his rule just before his assassination in 336 BCE. Young Alexander grew up in Athens, in the shadow not only of his father but also of the great philosopher Aristotle, who was his teacher. He succeeded his father at age twenty, already a man destined for greatness. Although Alexander ruled for only thirteen years, he was able to build an empire greater than any other that had yet existed. After he defeated **Darius III (c. 380–330 BCE)** in the **Battle of Issus** in 333 BCE, the Persian Empire crumbled. By the time he was thirty-three, Alexander ruled over fifty times more land and twenty times the number of people that had existed in the empire he inherited from Philip. This territory included Greece, Egypt, the former Persian Empire, and the Middle East, as we know it today. He had marched as far north as the Danube and as far east as the Ganges in India, and he had even sent an expedition to find the source of the Nile River. Upon his death in 323 BCE, he was considered the greatest general and empire-builder the world had ever known. Even today, almost twenty-four centuries later, he has barely half a dozen rivals to this achievement.

However, the true importance of Alexander's empire was that, for the first time, there could be a free exchange of ideas between two different cultures. Unlike most other victorious leaders, Alexander was not only receptive to the ideas of his conquered peoples but he also adopted ideas he learned from Persian political organization. On the other hand, Greek art influenced the art of India. Before his untimely death of natural causes at age thirty-three, Alexander also built the city of **Alexandria** in Egypt, whose great library, which evolved into the greatest center of learning in the world, survived for a thousand years.

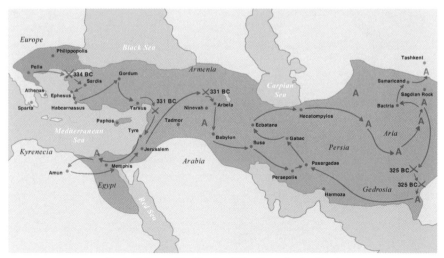

Routes taken and battles fought by Alexander the Great

BEFORE THE beginning of recorded history, when people formed themselves into groups, or bands, a single figure emerged as the leader. He was able to lead because of a distinct mixture of intelligence and power that we call leadership. As the nomadic bands ceased wandering and built cities, leaders became omnipotent and separate from the people they ruled. Most rulers were seen as having divine powers. In Egypt, for example, the pharaohs were accepted as gods. The authority of kings was enormous, and they typically ruled by decree. What the king dictated became the law of the land. Some rulers were benevolent and some were arbitrarily cruel, but most ruled with an iron fist.

In India, there lived a king named **Asoka (?–232 BCE)**, who ruled the kingdom of Magadha from 273 BCE to 232 BCE. His empire eventually came to include almost all of what is India today, as well as what is now Pakistan and Bangladesh. In 261 BCE, his armies crushed the **Kalingas** in a particularly bloody war, which had up to 200,000 casualties. As a witness to the horror and suffering, Asoka was appalled and decided that no military victory was worth such a cost. He converted to Buddhism and renounced military conquest as a national policy. He banned animal and human sacrifice and retained his army in a solely defensive posture.

However, beyond simply reacting to the violence of aggressive foreign policy, Asoka also reformulated his domestic policy to include public works projects and the establishment of institutions that would serve the welfare of the people he governed. Asoka had become a man with a conscience, and possibly the world's first truly "enlightened" monarch.

Asoka

◆ **CHINA, LIKE** Europe before and after the peak of the Roman Empire's power, was a conglomeration of politically divergent feudal city-states ruled by rival warlords. These states were united only by a generally common culture that had emerged during the Chou dynasty, which had existed in the Yangtze River Valley after 770 BCE and had exerted a lasting cultural, if not political, influence on the rest of China.

The greatest influence on Chinese culture during this period—and perhaps ever—were the writings of the philosopher **Kung-fu-tzu (551–479 BCE)**, also known by his Latin name, **Confucius**. His philosophy, which over six million people still follow as a religion, stressed the importance of a harmonious social order on a national, as well as personal, level.

After his death, China disintegrated politically into the **Warring States Period (about 475–221 BCE)**. This period ended with the advent of the **Ch'in dynasty (221–207 BCE)**, during which the powerful **Shih-huang-ti (259–210 BCE)**—known as the "First Emperor"—succeeded in uniting China for the first time in history. He introduced a centralized government, conducted a census, and standardized the country's coinage, written language, laws, and weights and measures. He also began work on the **Great Wall of China**, the largest engineering project ever accomplished by human hands prior to the middle of the nineteenth century. On the downside, Shih-huang-ti is remembered as an authoritarian despot who undertook a concerted effort to stamp out Confucianism, an objective that was only partially successful.

Shih-huang-ti's rule was superseded by the **Han dynasty**, which benefited by his centralization but gradually reintroduced Confucianism. The Han dynasty went on to establish the **Mandarin** social and political system, which survived as the basis

Shih-huang-ti

of Chinese society even under the **Ch'ing (Manchu) dynasty (1644–1912)** until the Communists seized power in 1949. The Han dynasty itself lasted over four hundred years, until 220 CE. During this time, the arts and sciences—from literature and painting, to astronomy and mathematics—flourished widely.

ROME WAS founded in 753 BCE, but it would be five hundred years before the Romans asserted their influence beyond the Italian peninsula; however, in those five centuries, the city on the Tiber River had become the dominant political force in Italy. As its sphere of influence spread outside Italy, Rome would face new and more serious competition than it had closer to home.

While Greece looked east toward the cradle of civilization and the Persian Empire beyond, Rome looked west. The major power in the western Mediterranean was **Carthage**, a city founded in 814 BCE by the Phoenicians. As Rome began to broaden its sphere of power, it put itself on a collision course with Carthage. The victor in this power struggle would win dominance over Western Europe and ultimately the entire Mediterranean area. The contest was decided during the course of the **Punic Wars**. The word "punic" is derived from the Latin word *Punicus,* meaning Carthaginian, which itself is derived from the Greek word *Phoinix,* meaning Phoenician. The **First Punic War (264–241 BCE)** was waged primarily at sea and resulted in a Roman victory. The **Second Punic War (219–201 BCE)** involved one of the most amazing campaigns in military history. In this action, the Carthaginian general **Hannibal (247–182 BCE)** defeated Rome's allies in what is now Spain in 219 BCE and set out to strike Rome itself. He crossed the Alps with his armies in 218 BCE and scored a series of victories in northern Italy. Meanwhile, the Roman general **Scipio (236–183 BCE)** outflanked Hannibal. He recaptured Spain and set out to besiege Carthage itself, even as Hannibal arrived at the gates of Rome. Hannibal returned to Carthage to protect the city and lost to Scipio on the **Plain of Zama** on October 19, 202 BCE.

The **Third Punic War (149–146 BCE)**, during which Carthage was captured and completely destroyed by the Romans, was anticlimactic. The Roman victory at the Battle of Zama in 202 BCE marked the beginning of the power of the Roman Empire that would continue to reign supreme for six centuries.

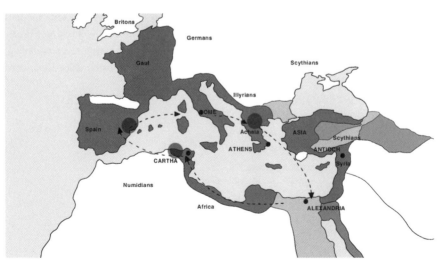

The Romans captured Carthage in the Third Punic War, expanding their empire

◆ **IMMORTALIZED IN** story and verse and on the Shakespearean stage, **Julius Caesar (100–44 BCE)** is remembered as the quintessential Roman emperor; however, Rome was still a republic when he was alive, and the emperor's office wasn't created until after his death. With the defeat of Carthage in the Punic Wars, Rome came to think of itself as having a "manifest destiny" to subjugate and rule as much of the known world as possible. Julius Caesar was the agent of Rome who realized this manifest destiny. He pushed the frontiers of the Roman Empire farther than any Roman emperor.

As the son of a noble family, Caesar entered the Roman army, served with distinction, and earned the Civic Crown, the highest medal of valor. Upon his return to Rome, he entered politics, becoming state treasurer at age thirty-four. He was elected to a consulship nine years later. He introduced many important reforms and became very popular, but his eyes were clearly fixed on the singular role of absolute ruler. In order to achieve this goal, Caesar decided that he needed to enhance his popularity by heading a successful military expedition to expand the empire.

He took command of an army and succeeded in conquering Gaul (today's France) by 55 BCE. Over the course of the next two years, he invaded and laid claim to most of Britain and crossed the Rhine River to fight the Germans. He returned to Rome as a powerful hero but encountered a political conflict with **Pompey (106–48 BCE)**, the Roman general who had captured Jerusalem and who held the post of Chief Consul. Caesar demanded the consulship, but Pompey denied him. By law, generals were not allowed to bring their armies into the city of Rome but were required to keep them north of the Rubicon River. In

Julius Caesar

50 BCE, Caesar flouted the law, crossed the Rubicon, and entered Rome to stage a coup. He deposed Pompey and eliminated the republic, making himself an absolute ruler as he had planned. He continued to rule until he was assassinated by disgruntled colleagues on March 15, 44 BCE.

Julius Caesar altered the course of Roman and European history. In Rome, he overthrew the republic and created the office of a de facto emperor, which his nephew, **Octavian (63 BCE–14 CE)**, would make official when he took power fourteen years after his uncle's death. When Caesar's rule began, Rome was the major power in the Mediterranean. By the time of his death, Rome had also become Europe's—and possibly the world's—first superpower.

BEFORE JULIUS CAESAR was assassinated in 44 BCE, he had enlarged the boundaries of what was a de facto **Roman Empire**, and he had become Rome's first absolute ruler. Yet the Roman Empire was not officially declared until Caesar's nephew, **Octavian (63 BCE–14 CE)**, took power in 27 BCE.

Although Caesar had named Octavian as his successor, he faced opposition from both his uncle's supporters and rivals. Octavian agreed to rule as part of a

The Temple of Jupiter Capitolinus in Ancient Rome

triumvirate (a three-man ruling council) with **Marcus Lepidus (?–13 BCE)** and **Mark Antony (83–30 BCE)**, one of Caesar's trusted lieutenants. This triumvirate, in turn, faced a civil war brought about by **Gaius Cassius (?–42 BCE)** and **Marcus Junius Brutus (85–42 BCE)**, two of the conspirators in Caesar's assassination who wanted to reestablish the republic. After their defeat, the triumvirate divided their rule geographically, with Octavian in Europe, Lepidus in Africa, and Antony in Egypt.

In Egypt, where the local monarchy was subjected to Roman rule, Mark Antony set up the seat of power in the cosmopolitan city of Alexandria where he fell in love with and married the Egyptian queen, Cleopatra **(69–30 BCE)**. He named their three children as his successors and frequently gave his wife lavish presents, which spawned a rumor that he planned to give her Rome as a gift. When word of this rumor reached Octavian, he became infuriated and declared war. The two sides met in the **Battle of Actium in 31 BCE**, where the armies of Antony and Cleopatra were

defeated. They escaped to Egypt with the remnants of their forces, but Octavian was in close pursuit. Sensing that their cause was hopeless, both Antony and Cleopatra committed suicide in 30 BCE. Octavian declared himself as the Roman emperor, taking the name **Caesar Augustus**.

Actium was a turning point for Rome and for world history. If Octavian had lost, the center of world power would have shifted from Rome to Alexandria, and the character of the empire would have changed dramatically. It would have become the cosmopolitan tapestry that **Alexander the Great** had envisioned for his empire, rather than the tightly disciplined and centrally controlled monarchy that it became under Octavian. The **Latin** language and the Roman alphabet would not have become the standard for all of Europe, and Christianity probably would not have spread as widely and successfully as it subsequently did.

Rome had been an empire before Octavian became Caesar Augustus, but it was he who proclaimed it to be *the* Roman Empire, and it was he who presided over a period when *Pax Romana* (the peace of Rome) reigned throughout the "known world." Thus began Rome's golden age. United under a single powerful leader, the empire began to flourish culturally and commercially. Art and literature began to become an important part of life in Roman cities. Massive construction projects were undertaken to build roads, bridges, aqueducts, coliseums, apartment houses, and public buildings in the city of Rome and throughout the empire.

BORN IN 4 BCE in Bethlehem in what was then Roman Palestine, **Jesus Christ** inspired what came to be one of the world's most widely followed religions. Today, there are more than 2.5 billion Christians, accounting for nearly one-third of the world's people. The Jewish tradition—into which Jesus was born—was unique among ancient religions in its belief that there was one God. The Jews further believed that their one God—known as Jehovah—would send a **Messiah**, or Savior, to deliver them from Roman rule as Moses had delivered them from Egyptian slavery in about 1250 BCE. Christians not only believe that Jesus *is* the Messiah but also that he is the Son of God who was sent to die for the people in order for them to be reborn in God's grace and have access to eternal paradise, or heaven. To the followers of **Christianity**, the birth of Jesus Christ was the pivotal event of world history.

Christians adopted Jewish scriptures for the period prior to 4 BCE, and these form the **Old Testament** of the Christian Bible. The two traditions diverge at that point, as Jews do not accept Jesus Christ as *the* Messiah. The **New Testament** of the Christian Bible contains a record of Christ's own teachings as recorded by his disciples, mainly **Matthew**, **Mark**, **Luke**, and **John**.

Jesus was born to Mary and her husband Joseph, a young carpenter from Nazareth, in Roman Palestine. Orthodox Christians believe that Joseph was simply Jesus's stepfather because Jesus was, literally, the Son of God. Jesus began teaching when he was twenty-nine years of age. He was introduced to the people of the region by his cousin John (**St. John the Baptist, 5 BCE–30 CE**), a prophet who identified Jesus as the Son of God and the Messiah. Jesus's most well-known message, the **Sermon on the Mount**, summarizes the essence of Christian belief in a moral code that teaches the importance

Jesus Christ is often depicted as a shepherd

of peace, honesty, simplicity, tolerance, and meekness.

During the three to four years that he was preaching in Palestine, Jesus worked many miracles and gathered many followers. He also made enemies in official circles among those who saw the charismatic young preacher as a threat to their authority. In 29 or 30 CE, Jesus was arrested in Jerusalem and sentenced to death by the Roman prosecutor Pontius Pilate. Jesus was nailed to a cross on a hill called Calvary and left to die.

According to Christian belief, his body—united with his soul—rose from the dead three days later, and he appeared to his followers many times over the next forty days. These followers then set out to preach his words to the people of the Roman Empire and the world beyond.

IN THE three centuries after the death of **Caesar Augustus** in 14 CE, imperial Rome flourished as no society had before. Except for occasional border skirmishes, the Roman Empire was secure, and its military power unchallenged. *Pax Romana* prevailed.

It was against this backdrop of civil order and relative peace that Christianity began to grow and expand. Unlike previous religions, which were handed down through the generations as a feature of one's culture, Christianity actively sought to convert others. It took root in the Middle East and spread to Greece and Egypt. Christian missionaries, particularly Jesus's friend **Peter (?–64 CE)**, the patriarch of Christianity, along with **Saul of Tarsus (4–c. 62 CE)**, now known as **St. Paul**, carried word of the new faith to all parts of the empire and even to Rome itself.

At first, Christianity was tolerated by the Romans, but as it became more widespread and perceived as a threat to Roman unity, emperors began to persecute the Christians. The ugly spectacle of Christians being thrown to the lions in Rome's Coliseum for the amusement of Roman crowds became a familiar sight.

Nevertheless, Rome became the headquarters of the Christian Church, which at first was an underground movement. This changed over time, and by the beginning of the fourth century, **Emperor Constantine (280–337 CE)** had embraced Christianity. Once Constantine became emperor in 306 CE, Christianity was accepted and even promoted. Constantine even went so far as to mediate a major internal dispute over doctrine between the eastern and western factions of the Church. He invited the bishops representing the two groups to a huge conference in **Nicaea** in 325 CE, at which their differences were resolved. The **Nicene**

Emperor Constantine

Creed, drafted at this meeting, set out the basic Christian beliefs upon which both sides could agree.

Constantine took steps to save Christianity from being destroyed by both external persecution and internal strife, and he established Christianity as a de facto state religion throughout the Roman Empire. Constantine not only preserved Christianity, but by making it the Roman Empire's *official* religion, he also took an all-important step that helped make Christianity the dominant religion in Europe, which it has been ever since. Had he not done this, the cultural history of Europe would have been vastly different.

BY THE end of the fourth century, the Romans began to experience great difficulties managing their far-flung empire, which stretched from Britain to the Black Sea and included every mile of the Mediterranean shoreline. The time needed to travel or send messages from one remote part of the realm to another was tremendous. Edicts, or laws, issued from Rome could take months to reach outlying locations. Control and communications, which had always been tenuous, eventually began to disintegrate. Tribes from northern Europe, such as the **Goths**, the **Visigoths**, the **Vandals**, and the **Franks**, had conducted forays against the borders of the empire for years, and such attacks only increased. Even Italy fell prey to attacks by the "barbarians."

Early in the fourth century, **Emperor Constantine (280–337 CE)** decided Rome was not safe, and he moved the capital to the ancient city of **Byzantium** (now Istanbul), which he renamed **Constantinople**. When Constantine died in 337 CE, his sons divided and then squabbled over the empire. The result was a division of the empire into an **Eastern Roman Empire**, based in Constantinople, and a **Western Roman Empire**, based in Rome.

As the Western Roman Empire began to crumble under its own weight, northern Europeans gradually began to conquer pieces of it until they controlled large portions of Italy. **Alaric (370–410 CE)**, chief of the Visigoths, invaded and sacked Rome in 410 CE, and **Attila the Hun (406?–453 CE)** attacked the Roman provinces in the north around 434 CE. When the last Roman emperor, **Romulus Augustulus (c. fifth century CE)**, was elected in 475 CE, he presided over a tiny shadow of the once invincible Roman Empire. When he was taken prisoner at Ravenna in 476 CE by the German **King Odovacar (433–493 CE)**, the sun finally set on the empire that Caesar Augustus decreed 505 years before.

The Roman Empire at its peak

TODAY, ISLAM is the second most widely held religious belief, with nearly two billion faithful, accounting for 24 percent of the world's people. Like Judaism and Christianity, Islam is monotheistic. The followers of Islam believe in one God, whom they call **Allah** (meaning "God" in Arabic). As the Muslims say when reciting the Shahada (an Islamic oath), "There is no god but Allah and Muhammad is the messenger of God."

Muhammad, the founder of Islam, was born around 570 CE near **Mecca**, in what is now Saudi Arabia. His parents died when he was young, and Muhammad was raised by other family members. When he was still a boy, he traveled throughout the Middle East with his uncle, who was a trader. He encountered many different people and became familiar with their ideas and customs. He was attracted to the Judeo-Christian idea of monotheism. In 610 CE, while he was meditating near Mecca, he began to have a series of visions in which God instructed him to preach monotheism to the polytheistic peoples of the Arabian Peninsula. He also began to write the **Koran**, Islam's sacred scripture.

As he gained disciples, authorities in Mecca began to perceive him as a threat to their authority. Finally, they surrounded Muhammad and many of his followers in one corner of the city and threatened to let them starve to death unless Muhammad retracted what he had been preaching and his followers abandoned Muhammad and monotheism. Meanwhile, two rival factions in neighboring **Medina** had taken an interest in Muhammad and his beliefs and invited him to come there. He escaped from Mecca on July 16, 622 CE and went to Medina. This date of Muhammad's journey, or **hejira**, marks the beginning of Islam.

Embraced by the rulers of Medina, Muhammad raised an army to use in spreading Islamic beliefs to rival tribes. He returned to conquer Mecca in 630 CE, and by the time of his death in 632 CE, his armies had converted most of the people on the Arabian Peninsula. Within ten years of his death, this process had been extended by force to Persia, Egypt, and throughout the Middle East. By the middle of the eighth century, the territory controlled both politically and religiously by the Islamic Empire stretched from Spain, across North Africa, through the Middle East, and deep into central Asia.

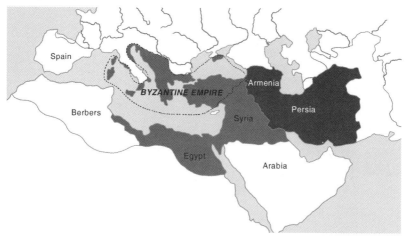

Islam spread quickly during the seventh century BCE

IN THE centuries after the collapse of the Roman Empire in 476 CE, fragments of the former whole became individual power centers ruled by notable monarchs whose names are now legendary. **Theodoric the Great (454–526 CE)** ruled the Ostrogothic Kingdom of Italy; **Clovis (466–511 CE)** presided over the Franks in what is now France; **Justinian the Great (483–565 CE)** reigned in Byzantium over the former Eastern Roman Empire; and **King Arthur (?–537 CE)** held court at Camelot in Britain.

Charlemagne

However, when Europe lost the unity of the Roman Empire and became a patchwork of squabbling kingdoms, it took a step backward culturally. Thus began the **Middle Ages**, or as they were once described, the **Dark Ages**.

Except for Spain, which was ruled by the Islamic **Moors**, Europe was fragmented politically but unified religiously by the bond of Christianity. While the home of the Christian popes in Rome remained the spiritual center of Europe, the **Franks** in northern Europe emerged as the strongest military and secular power. By the end of the eighth century, their most powerful leader was the twenty-six-year-old **Charlemagne (747–814 CE)** (the French word for Charles the Great), who lived from 742 to 814 CE and is now considered to be one of the greatest rulers in European history. His greatest opposition was from the Italian king, **Desiderius**, who wanted **Pope Adrian I (?–795 CE)** to crown the underage children of Charlemagne's predecessor as monarchs of segments of the kingdom of the Franks.

After Charlemagne defeated Desiderius, he consolidated most of the northern Italian states under Frank control. Charlemagne then went to Rome to meet with the pope and found that their long-range strategies were quite compatible. Charlemagne's goal was to become head of an empire on the scale of the old Roman Empire, and Adrian I wanted one dominant, unified, political force to rule Europe that would ally itself with the Church and could serve to protect and expand Christendom the way the Moorish armies were spreading Islam.

With the spiritual and political blessing of the pope, Charlemagne added much of Denmark, Germany, and central Europe to an empire that already included France and most of Italy. He also recaptured part of Spain from the Moors. On Christmas Day in 800 CE, while he was attending Mass in Rome, Charlemagne unexpectedly found himself being crowned "Emperor of the Romans" by Adrian's successor, **Pope Leo III (751–816 CE)**. The Western Roman Empire, which had not existed for 325 years, was back in business, this time as the *Holy Roman Empire* (though it was not yet *officially* known as such). Although he was not recognized by the emperor of the Eastern Roman Empire until 812 CE, Charlemagne quickly won the respect of most of the peoples of his empire, enabling Europe to once again experience the *Pax Romana* as a unified and basically peaceful environment. Because of this, Charlemagne's rule can be said to have been a moment of sunshine in the midst of the darkness of the Dark Ages.

◆ **CHARLEMAGNE'S EMPIRE** was inherited by his intended successor, **Louis the Pious (778–840 CE)**. After Louis died, infighting among his sons caused the empire to collapse into pieces. This void was filled by the Catholic Church, which began to assert increasing political, as well as spiritual, power.

Europe, however, had begun to sink back into the Dark Ages. The disunity that preceded Charlemagne's brilliant rule had returned. Both Italy and France were a morass of warring factions, but among the Germans, a new leader emerged. **Henry I (876?–936 CE)**, known as "The Fowler," was a forceful leader who consolidated the German states, leaving to his son and successor, **Otto I (912–973 CE)**, a formidable power base.

Otto I sought to bring unity to the lands that had once composed Charlemagne's vast empire. Again, as it had been with Charlemagne, Otto's authority sprang from the pope's desire for a strong northern Europe that would restore order in Italy. Pope John XII was at war with the Italian king, **Berengar (900?–966 CE)**, and offered Otto the crown and title of **Holy Roman Emperor** if he would defeat Berengar and unite the peninsula. This accomplished, Otto I was crowned on February 2, 962 CE.

The idea of a **Holy Roman Empire** had been born with Charlemagne and now it was reborn with Otto I. Charlemagne's empire survived his death by only twenty-seven years.

The Holy Roman Empire would survive Otto's death by more than eight centuries. The Holy Roman Empire essentially consisted of the present territory of Germany, Austria, Italy, the Czech Republic, and some adjacent territory. It would continue to wield might and power until the fifteenth century, and it would survive in name until 1806.

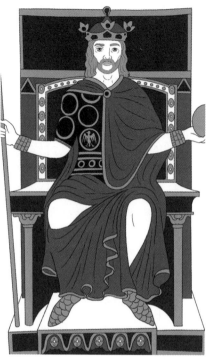

Otto I

Just as it was intended, the Holy Roman Empire brought political as well as spiritual union to the heart of Europe by bringing many diverse peoples together. In the centuries that followed, all the superpowers that appeared were outside of the Holy Roman Empire. These were England, France, and Spain.

However, the autonomy that remained in individual kingdoms prevented the emergence of a true power center within the Holy Roman Empire.

ENGLAND AT the peak of its power in the nineteenth century controlled the largest empire the world has ever known. Yet in the days of the Roman Empire, it was still a wild frontier. The **Celtic** peoples of the British Isles were fiercely independent; nevertheless, they were subjugated by the Romans until the fifth century and by the **Anglo-Saxons** thereafter. The Vikings had also established a foothold by the fifth century. By the ninth century, Anglo-Saxons predominated and ruled for nearly six hundred years, except for a span of twenty-six years when the British Isles were under Danish domination.

In 1066, **King Harold II (1020–1066)** succeeded his brother-in-law **Edward the Confessor (1002–1066)** as king of England. Edward had promised the throne to Harold publicly, but it was not an easy transition. Edward's half brother, **William of Normandy (1027–1087)**, also laid claim to the title by showing evidence that Harold had promised to support him as king of England.

William gathered an army of Normans and Frenchmen, crossed the English Channel from Normandy, which is in the north of France, and invaded England. Harold, failing to disrupt his landing, met William in battle at **Hastings** on October 14, 1066. Harold's troops, which were on foot, were a poor match for the heavily armed and armored Normans, who were mounted on horseback. William's cavalry also outmaneuvered the Saxon infantry, and by the end of the day, Harold and many of his officers were dead, their armies defeated.

On Christmas Day, William was crowned king of England and was henceforth known as **William the Conqueror**. Although both Napoleon and Hitler tried to duplicate his momentous victory, William was the last man in history to head a victorious invasion of England by a force of arms.

The Battle of Hastings was fought between the armies of King Harold II and William the Conqueror

With the Norman Conquest, England was opened to the influences of European art and literature. Although England retained its English language, it filtered and adopted the best that Europe had to offer. This basic building block of English civilization would, in turn, create and define that of North America.

◆ **AFTER THE** fall of the Western Roman Empire in 475 CE, the Eastern Roman Empire continued to control access to Christian holy places in **Jerusalem** and **Bethlehem**. In 610 CE, however, the Persians, who ruled until 630 CE, captured Jerusalem. At the same time, Muhammad continued spreading Islam by force, and his followers seized Jerusalem in 638 CE. By the early eighth century, they had conquered the shores of the Mediterranean, from Spain to Constantinople. They did continue to tolerate Christian pilgrims who wanted to visit the holy places, and Charlemagne even formed an alliance with the caliph **Harun al-Rashid (764?–809 CE)**.

In 1071, Eastern emperor **Romanus Diogenes** declared war on the Turks and lost. This led to a collapse of the Eastern Empire and general chaos throughout the Middle East as rival Arab caliphs and Turkish sultans jockeyed for jurisdiction of the remnants. At this time, the Turks effectively cut off access to the Holy Land to European Christians. In 1095, at the **Council of Clermont**, **Pope Urban II (1035–1099)** called upon the knights of Christendom—such as those in France and the Holy Roman Empire—to raise an army that could reclaim the Holy Land. The first attempt in 1096 was poorly organized and a disastrous failure. Undaunted, the crusaders returned in 1097, and two years later they recaptured Jerusalem. The kingdom of Jerusalem was declared in 1099, and the **First Crusade** was deemed a success.

The kingdom of Jerusalem endured for forty-five years, but in 1144 it was overrun by the Turks. The **Second Crusade** failed in 1145, as did the **Third Crusade** in 1189. The **Fourth Crusade** between 1200 and 1204 did not succeed in securing Jerusalem, but the French knights did capture Orthodox Constantinople and establish a Roman Christian kingdom there that survived until 1262.

The crusades were a response by Christians to the spread of Islam

None of the next four Crusades, which took place between 1212 and 1270, succeeded as the First Crusade had and were for the most part utter failures. The most tragic crusade was probably the **Children's Crusade** of 1212. Only 201 of the 50,000 children who went to the Holy Land survived to return home.

The historic importance of the Crusades to Europe was not that they represented a series of military defeats, but the fact that they brought Europe in contact with the East. Although they failed to permanently liberate Jerusalem from Turkish control, the Crusades did succeed in opening a new world and providing a widened perspective for Europeans. In fact, many believe that the Crusades were the catalyst that ultimately led to the **Renaissance**.

THROUGHOUT HISTORY, there had been good monarchs and bad. There had been kind, benevolent monarchs and mean-spirited, vindictive ones. But until the thirteenth century, there had been, for the most part, only absolute monarchs. Even in the case of such enlightened monarchs as **Hammurabi** and **Asoka**, the king was the king, and his decree was the law of the land. Essentially, all laws in Europe, except those decreed by the Church, were handed down from the king at his own discretion. He could levy taxes as he saw fit and jail anyone who dared to criticize him.

A particularly cruel ruler was **King John of England (1167–1216)** who succeeded his brother, **Richard the Lionhearted (1157–1199)**, in 1199. John was greedy, distrustful, and incompetent. He failed in his efforts to preserve England's dominions in France, and he succeeded in angering everyone from Pope Innocent II to the English people, as well as the English noblemen whom he taxed mercilessly. Those opposed to John's rule came from every walk of life. Finally, the noblemen and landowners gave him an ultimatum, insisting that he agree to their demands for more control over the government, which they were supporting by the payment of taxes. By mobilizing their considerable power and influence, they were finally able to compel the king to pay attention to their demands.

Reluctantly, King John met them at a field near Windsor called **Runnymede** on June 15, 1215, and was presented with their **Magna Carta (Great Charter)**. The charter, which they asked the king to sign, was a sixty-three–part compendium of rights, which should be granted to "free men."

"I will never grant such liberties as will make *me* a slave!" King John hissed. But

King John of England signing the Magna Carta

he signed under duress, as the nobles had given him no choice.

The Magna Carta is still recognized as the foundation of the English legal system and other legal systems in many parts of the world—including North America. It stipulated numerous rights, which protected the individual, including the right to a jury trial, that punishment should fit the crime, and that taxes should be based on fairness and proportion. However, the most important, lasting accomplishment of the **Magna Carta** was that it made sure the king was no longer *above* the law but would be held accountable to the laws and customs of the land just like any other citizen.

IN THE thirteenth century, people in China only had the vaguest idea that people in Europe even existed, and vice versa. Yet all would come to be terrified of one man. He and his "Hordes" seemed to come out of nowhere, instilling fear in people from one end of the earth to the other.

Genghis Khan (1162–1227), a Mongol warlord who had little use for the finer things of Chinese or European civilization, slept in a yurt, and rode a fast, sturdy Mongolian stallion, evolved into perhaps the most successful military leader in the history of the world. Late in the twelfth century, he became the leader of a Mongol band who saw no limit to the potential size of a **Mongol Empire**.

Genghis Khan

The Mongols were a nomadic people who lived on the vast plains of central Asia. For many years, they eked out a living on the steppes, fighting among themselves and raiding villages on the fringes of the Chinese Empire. Few people beyond the periphery of their homeland had even heard of them. The **Great Wall of China**, begun around 200 BCE, generally kept them at bay, and most of Europe was several thousand miles from the cold, high deserts the Mongols inhabited. Eventually, neither wall nor distance would matter.

Genghis first turned his attention to the **Tatars**. Having defeated them, he plunged south into China, where the **Jin dynasty** was on the brink of ruin and hence an easy target for the marauding Mongols. Genghis captured Beijing in 1215 and soon occupied most of China. In 1219, he looked west toward lands that had not yet heard of his conquests.

The "Mongol Hordes," as the vast oceans of heavily armed horsemen came to be known, swept across Russia, digested the **Persian Empire**, swallowed Poland and Hungary, and threatened all of Europe. Over the next eight years, Genghis amassed the largest contiguous empire the world had yet seen. Only the British Empire, when it included both Canada and Australia, would be larger. Unlike Alexander the Great, the Caesars, or the Persian emperors, Genghis Khan's idea of conquest was not to occupy and rule another people, but rather to rape, pillage, and destroy everything in his path. His total disregard for human life led to his being utterly dreaded throughout virtually the entire Eurasian land mass.

However, the success of the Hordes was completely dependent on Genghis Khan's leadership abilities and his unification of the Mongols. When **Ogadai Khan (1185–1241)** succeeded him and continued on a path of conquest, the Mongol juggernaut eventually ran out of steam, and the Hordes returned to central Asia.

In the long run, the most important impact that the Mongol Empire had on history was that it made people at opposite ends of the globe—China and Europe—aware of one another. The Crusades had reopened the ancient dialogue between Europe and the *Middle* East, but before the Mongols, Europeans were largely unaware that the Far East existed.

UNTIL THE thirteenth century, the impression Europeans had of Asia was based on their horrible experience with the Mongols, and they possessed little knowledge of the complex Chinese culture, which lay beyond Mongolia. Because there had been virtually no interaction between the cultures, they did not know enough about each other to want to open a dialogue. Their alphabets, language, and cultural traditions evolved independently and were decidedly different.

Marco Polo meeting with Kublai Khan

Few Europeans had heard of China, and none had journeyed there and back to tell the tale until **Niccolò Polo** and his brother **Maffeo Polo** did so in 1269.

The two brothers from the Italian city-state of Venice—one of the most important trading cities in Europe—had traveled to the Black Sea on a trading mission where they met some people from **Turkestan** (later the Central Asian republics of the USSR). Through them, the Italians met envoys from the court of **Kublai Khan (1215–1294)**, the Mongol emperor of China. The Chinese invited the Polo brothers to visit China and meet their emperor, who had never seen a European. Kublai Khan, who was very interested in what they had to say, told them to ask the pope to send missionaries to instruct the Chinese people in Christianity and art and literature of Europe.

When the brothers returned to Italy in 1269, their fellow countrymen could not grasp the enormity of their story. In 1271, they decided to return to China, and this time they took Niccolò's teen-age son, Marco. Kublai Khan took a liking to the young man and made him an ambassador at large, sending him on many missions within China, as well as to Tibet and Burma. **Marco Polo (1254?–1324)** saw more of Asia than any European had ever seen, or even had dreamed of seeing.

Along with his father and uncle, Marco stayed in China for over twenty years. He learned the languages and customs of Asia and met many of its diverse peoples. When the Polos returned to Venice in 1295, they once again met with skepticism, but after they demonstrated what they had learned in China, their fellow Venetians were finally convinced, and the Polos were welcomed and honored.

Many of the wondrous things that they brought back from China had never been seen in Europe before. There is even a tale—unproven—that they introduced spaghetti to Italy from China. Marco's book, *The Travels of Marco Polo,* is perhaps the most famous and influential travel book in history. With its wealth of detail, it provided medieval Europe its first substantial account of China and other Asian countries.

Because traveling overland was difficult, trade between Europe and the Far East was slow in developing, but the way was opened after Marco Polo published the details of a workable trade route. Indeed, Christopher Columbus's voyage two centuries later was inspired by a desire to find an easier route to China.

IN THE centuries before the widespread use of antibiotics in the twentieth century, disease was rampant and epidemics were not uncommon. The life expectancy of the average human was less than forty years, and the infant mortality rate was much higher than today. Nevertheless, the **plague**, or **"Black Death,"** that struck Europe in the middle of the fourteenth century was a medical disaster unequaled in human history.

The bubonic plague was caused
by germs carried by fleas

Prior to the plague, the epidemics that occurred were usually fierce but short-lived. Most importantly, they had been confined to relatively small geographic areas. By contrast, the grip of the Black Death was relentless, and it spread throughout Europe, from Sicily to Sweden and from England to Spain.

The disease took its name from the way it manifested itself as blackish blood blisters that formed under the skin. The blisters were usually accompanied by a very high fever, intense pain, and swollen glands, eventually resulting in death. Incurable pneumonia or syphilis were frequently present. Because the cause of the disease remained unknown, it was widely believed to be an act of God. Clinically, however, the Black Death was actually **bubonic plague**, which is caused by *bacillus pestis* germs injected into the bloodstream by fleas carried by brown rats.

People everywhere went mad with fear. Some committed suicide. Others burned all their possessions in a vain attempt to stop the spread of the disease. The failure of religious invocations to stop the tide of the plague resulted in displeasure with the Church, and counter-religious activities, such as "Black Masses," began to appear.

Death estimates from the plague range from twenty-five to thirty-five million. As much as one-third of the total European population died between 1348 and 1350. Some smaller cities lost 90 percent of their people. Hamburg, Germany, lost up to two-thirds of its citizenry, and England may have lost up to half of its population. Entire families died, and many others were broken apart as other families adopted orphans.

The economy of Europe was altered dramatically. A profound labor shortage resulted in higher wages, a higher cost for goods, and runaway inflation. Many businesses went bankrupt and landowners lost their property because, in many cases, they had no one to tend their shops or work the fields. The labor-intensive feudal system began to disintegrate.

The plague was a cataclysm that changed the course of European history. It not only impacted Europe's economy, but its religious life as well. By showing that the Church was powerless in the face of the disease, the plague may well have hastened the **Protestant Reformation**.

Although the plague was less severe after 1350, it continued to persist for many years. So high was its death toll that it would be another two hundred years before Europe's population reached the level where it had been in 1347.

THE PRINTING of multiple copies of a specific document, such as the book you are now holding in your hands, is something we take for granted today as an essential element of written, or nonverbal, communication. However, during the five thousand years from the time that alphabets were first used until the middle of the fifteenth century, every written document created anywhere in the world—with the exception of a few in China—were originals. If multiple examples of an original manuscript were required, they had to be copied by hand, an enormous task that could take years. In Europe during the Middle Ages, many Christian monks devoted their entire life to making multiple copies of the Bible and other important documents.

Printing—the process of using mechanization to produce multiple copies of a written document—began with the idea of carving blocks to represent letters or words, inking them and then imprinting their images on paper and other materials. **Bi Sheng (Pi Cheng)** in China is generally recognized as the man who invented printing. In 1041, he printed his first documents using letters, which he had baked in clay and then formed into sentences. Bi Sheng's process was improved by Wang Zhen in 1298, who made his characters out of hardwood and went on to print books and even newspapers.

As European trade with China expanded and flourished over the next several centuries, the printing process became known in the West. In 1423, **Laurens Janszoon Coster (1370–1440)** of Holland experimented with printing in the Roman alphabet using metal characters to produce a clay printing plate. These methods were a great improvement over hand copying, but they were still unwieldy. In 1436, a thirty-nine-year-old German named **Johannes Gutenberg**

Johannes Gutenberg examining a page proof from his moveable type printing press

(1400–1468) began work on a machine—the printing press—that would make printing a much faster and more economical procedure. He adapted, or reinvented, Bi Sheng's idea of movable type; that is, the idea of hundreds of individual letters that could be combined in numerous ways to lay out an entire page. Gutenberg published the first mass-produced edition of the Bible in Mainz, Germany, in 1456, and within a few decades, there were presses in operation all over Europe.

Gutenberg may not have invented printing, but he was the catalyst that helped launch the greatest revolution in the history of human communication. The printing press would have greater impact than anything that had come before it and be more far-reaching than anything that would occur in the next five hundred years.

FEW EVENTS have shaped the history of humankind as did the arrival of **Christopher Columbus (1451–1506)** in the Americas. Columbus didn't "discover" America— there were up to nine million native people in the Western Hemisphere when he set foot upon the shore at San Salvador. However, Native Americans had no knowledge of the existence of an Eastern Hemisphere any more than the Europeans realized that the Americas

Christopher Columbus

existed. The two hemispheres were as different and independent as if they had actually existed on separate planets. Vikings, under the leadership of **Leif Ericson (970–1020 CE)** had settled briefly in Nova Scotia in 1000 CE, but they never realized that they had landed in another hemisphere. Columbus opened the way for the interaction between the two hemispheres.

Today, we know that the world is a sphere with major landmasses in the eastern and western hemispheres. Until Columbus's time, however, the accepted view in Europe was that the world was flat like a plate, and if you sailed far enough out on the ocean, you would fall off the edge. The "world"—the landmass upon which we lived—was surrounded by water, and that was that.

Columbus was born in Genoa, a port city in Italy, and was one of a growing number of people who believed that the world was a sphere and that one could travel east or west and eventually return to the starting point.

There was also a practical reason to prove this theory. By the fifteenth century, trade with the Far East, which was precipitated by the Venetian traders who followed Marco Polo's trail, was flourishing in Europe, but Polo's overland trade route was an extremely long and difficult journey. Navigators, like Columbus, who believed in the spherical world theory, were convinced they could reach the Far *East* by sailing *west.*

Columbus went in search of a government that would underwrite the cost of his adventure. He was turned down by Genoa, Venice, and Portugal. He turned next to **King Ferdinand V (1452–1516)** and **Queen Isabella (1451–1504)** of Castille in Spain, who agreed to commit three ships—the *Niña, Pinta,* and *Santa María*—and crews to the task. Columbus set sail on September 6, 1492, and, after a five-week voyage during which his sailors almost mutinied, the expedition made landfall at **San Salvador** in the West Indies on October 12.

He returned to Spain on March 15, 1493, and made subsequent voyages of colonization in 1493, 1500, and 1502. He died in poverty and neglect in 1506, still believing that he had reached Asia. His discoveries were treated with enthusiasm by the Spanish, who energetically undertook an exploration and colonization effort that would ultimately lead to a survey of most of the Western Hemisphere's eastern coast within a generation and the realization that Columbus had in fact discovered a "New World."

HISTORICALLY, THE RENAISSANCE was a period that lasted between twenty-five and fifty years and centered roughly on the year 1500. It can be characterized as the brilliant awakening of art, thought, and literature that pulled Europe from the intellectual darkness of the Middle Ages. It was not a natural evolutionary extension of the Middle Ages but a cultural revolution: a reaction to the rigidity of medieval thought and tradition.

By definition, the word "renaissance" implies a revival or resurgence. The period known as the Renaissance was viewed as a rediscovery of the enlightenment of the golden ages of Greek and Roman (regarded as "classical") civilization. In fact, while the Renaissance found many people reading classical literature and reconsidering classical thought, the true heart of the Renaissance involved a great deal of innovation and invention. Universities sprang up throughout Europe, and there was a sudden surge in the dissemination of ideas. **Johannes Gutenberg (1400–1468)** developed the practical printing press in 1450, and the publishing industry was born. One of the first bestselling authors was the witty Dutch scholar **Desiderius Erasmus (1466?–1536)** of Rotterdam, whose humanist ideas epitomized the broad-minded, forward thinking of the Renaissance.

Notwithstanding the printing press, it is amazing that the Renaissance happened so quickly and that it occurred throughout the whole of Europe. For example, many of the greatest names in the history of art were contemporaries. In Italy, there were **Sandro Botticelli (1445–1510), Michelangelo Buonarroti (1475–1564), Perugino (c. 1450–1523), Raphael (1483–1520), Tiziano Vecelli (Titian) (c. 1488–1576)**, and the great **Leonardo da Vinci (1452–1519)**. These artists helped to revolutionize art by studying the details of natural form and the intricacies of the interaction of light and shadow on that form.

North of the Alps, there was an equally impressive list of artists: **Hiëronymus Bosch (1450–1516), Lucas Cranach (1472–1553), Albrecht Dürer (1471–1528), Hans Holbein the Elder (1465–1524)**, and **Hans Memling (1430–1494)**. The Renaissance was not restricted to the visual arts. The Flemish composer **Josquin des Prez (c. 1450–1521)** composed his *Miserere mei, Deus,* which is considered to be the best early example of counterpoint.

All of these people were active *simultaneously* in 1492 when **Christopher Columbus (1451–1506)** made his epic first voyage, and Michelangelo and Dürer were still alive when the expedition mounted by **Ferdinand Magellan (1480–1521)** circumnavigated the globe. They paved the way for future generations of artists and composers.

In terms of science, a new generation of scholars born during, or immediately after, the Renaissance revolutionized the way people viewed the world. **Nicolaus Copernicus (1473–1543)** determined that the earth revolved around the sun, not vice versa as commonly believed. **Johannes Kepler (1571–1630)** explained the laws of planetary motion. While studying the heavens with his telescope, **Galileo Galilei (1564–1642)** discovered the moons of Jupiter and the rings of Saturn. **William Gilbert (1544–1603)** coined the term **"electricity"** in 1600. **Andreas Vesalius (1514–1564)** was the first to employ modern surgical techniques.

The Renaissance was a milestone because it suddenly and profoundly affected the course of so many aspects of the history of Western art and culture.

UPON THE death of Jesus Christ, his disciples went out into the world armed with nothing but his words and his ideas. In the early years, Christians faced hardship and persecution, but by 325 CE, Christianity had become the official religion of both Roman empires. Over the ensuing centuries, the Roman Church gradually came to wield political as well as spiritual power, filling the void left by the collapse of the Western Roman Empire.

Unchecked power often breeds corruption, and so it was with the Church. Despite the presence of pious and intellectually distinguished churchmen, there were widespread abuses, not the least of which was the selling of indulgences—when a believer was promised that a payment of money to the Church would allow him to escape the wrath of God's judgment. During the **Inquisition** in Spain, those who held beliefs considered heretical, according to Church policy, were tortured and killed.

Martin Luther

By the fourteenth century, honorable religious men, such as **John Wycliffe (1320–1384)** in England and **John (Jan) Huss (1374–1415)** in Prague, began to speak out against corrupt Church practices, and a growing undercurrent of discontent emerged within the Church itself. The situation finally came to a head on October 31, 1517, when an Augustinian friar named **Martin Luther (1483–1546)** posted a document on the door of the castle church in Wittenberg, Germany. This letter, entitled *The 95 Theses Against the Abuse of Indulgences,* accused Archbishop Albrecht of Mainz of fraud in the sale of indulgences (he was alleged to have pocketed the money). Luther also condemned the practice of selling indulgences in general.

Luther was charged with **heresy** (adhering to a set of beliefs or opinions contrary to official Church teaching) and **excommunicated** (deprived of his membership in the Church) in 1521. Nevertheless, his courage in defense of his point of view attracted a great deal of attention, especially in Germany, and many others followed his lead and broke away from the Church. They were called **Protestants** because of their general protest against the Roman Church. Luther himself organized a new religious movement, which embraced the teachings of Christianity but rejected the political authority of the Roman Church. While there would eventually be many Protestant groups, those who followed Luther's interpretation of Christianity called themselves **Lutherans**. Today, Lutheranism is the dominant religion in Scandinavia, much of Germany, and parts of North America.

The revolution launched by Martin Luther did not destroy the Roman Church, but actually may have saved it. By forcing Church officials to confront shortcomings in the Church, Luther not only created an alternate form of Christianity but also compelled Rome to curb its political abuses.

EUROPEAN HISTORY is filled with the rise or fall of political or economic powers. At the time of Columbus's discoveries, Spain and Portugal were on the threshold of becoming great trading nations much like the Phoenicians had been three thousand years before or as the British would become four hundred years later.

Spain moved quickly to exploit the New World. Portugal, meanwhile, was more interested in trade with the Far East and in taking advantage of the route around the southern tip of Africa pioneered in 1498 by the Portuguese mariner **Vasco da Gama (1460?–1524)**. Nevertheless, the Portuguese were swift to make claims in the Western Hemisphere. This led to the pope being asked to partition the New World between Spain and Portugal. Unfortunately for Portugal, since the geography of the Western Hemisphere remained largely unknown in 1494, the north–south demarcation line to which the two parties agreed gave Portugal only the easternmost part of the New World. This area later became Brazil, and today that nation remains the only country in the Western Hemisphere where Portuguese is the official language.

The Spanish expeditiously asserted their dominance over the rest of America south of the Caribbean as they sought to find **El Dorado**, the elusive—and probably mythical—"city of gold." In the course of their conquests, the Spanish **conquistadors** came into conflict with two of the most highly evolved civilizations in the New World: the **Aztec Empire** centered at

Vasco da Gama

Teotihuacan in Mexico, and the **Inca Empire** centered at **Tiahuanaco** south of Lake Titicaca in what is now Bolivia. Both of these cultures had existed for a thousand years, had built massive cities—Teotihuacan was the largest city in the world in 1500—and had mastered mathematics, astronomy, and other sciences. They had not, however, mastered the technology of sixteenth century European warfare.

Riding horses and carrying firearms—both unknown to Native Americans—a relatively small number of conquistadors under **Hernando Cortéz (1485–1547)** met and defeated the forces of the former Aztec leader **Montezuma (1466–1520)** at Teotihuacan on August 14, 1521. Cortéz's subsequent cruelty to the conquered Aztecs was matched only by that meted out by **Francisco Pizarro (1471–1541)** when he conquered the Incas in 1535.

These two defeats of Native American empires by the conquistadors were the first major conflicts between empires of the Old World and empires of the New World, and they were decisive. They put the New World's vast mineral wealth, particularly that of Mexico, at Spain's disposal, making Spain the most powerful nation on earth for the next one hundred years. Perhaps most of all, these victories encouraged Spain's thirst to expand its empire and led to it having the largest empire the Western Hemisphere would ever see. Today, five hundred million people in the Western Hemisphere speak Spanish.

DURING THE course of the sixteenth century, the New World Columbus "discovered" in 1492 was the object of a wave of European expeditions and efforts at colonization. The Spanish and the Portuguese were the first to divide the area south of the West Indies (the Portuguese received what is now Brazil and the Spanish nearly everything else). Explorer Hernando Cortéz gained a foothold in Mexico and plundered South America early in the sixteenth century. Later in the century, the Spanish

Pilgrims arriving in the New World

also landed in Florida, and the Dutch and French established outposts farther north in what is now the eastern part of the United States and Canada. Although their first colony in what is now the United States would not be established until after the beginning of the seventeenth century, the English subsequently made the greatest inroads into North America.

In 1497, **John Cabot (1450–1499)** was the first to explore the coast of North America for England, and **Sir Francis Drake (1540?–1596)** surveyed much of the Western Hemisphere's coastline after 1572. But the early English explorers were less interested in the New World itself than in finding a water trade route to China.

Another great English treasure hunter, **Sir Walter Raleigh (1554?–1618)**, hoped to find gold in North America as the Spanish had in South America, but he failed both in his efforts to locate gold and in his 1584–1587 attempts to start a permanent English colony. He did, however, claim a slice of the Atlantic coast for England, naming it Virginia for his friend and monarch Elizabeth I.

In 1607, the English finally planted the seed that evolved into the largest English-speaking nation in the world. **Captain John Smith (1579?–1631)** founded his settlement at **Jamestown** (named for King James I) in the territory of Virginia. The colony nearly failed several times, but the colonists held on, and in 1619, the people of Jamestown inaugurated the first representative assembly in North America: a precursor to the form of government that would later predominate.

Another settlement was established at Plymouth in 1620 in what is now Massachusetts by a group of British subjects who called themselves **Pilgrims**. Fleeing what they perceived as political persecution of their religious sect, the Pilgrims came to America in their ship the *Mayflower* to establish a colony in which they could worship as they wished without governmental interference. Plymouth was important because it was the first successful North American settlement founded by ordinary Europeans without a charter from a European government.

Over the course of the next three hundred years, a small band of determined settlers at Jamestown and Plymouth became the most powerful political and economic power in the world.

HE WAS probably the greatest scientific genius in the history of the world. He was certainly the greatest European scientist who lived between the time of Archimedes and Einstein. Before he was twenty-four, **Isaac Newton (1642–1727)** invented calculus, discovered the spectrum of light, and wrote his **theory of gravitation**. The latter allegedly occurred to him while he was watching an apple fall from a tree. It is a tribute to his genius that he was able to develop such a complex, universal theory from so commonplace an event.

Newton also invented the reflector telescope, which differed from the simpler refractor type in that the light reflected directly to the eye from a large, concave mirror via a small, flat mirror without passing through glass.

In 1667, when he was twenty-five, Newton was an elected fellow at Trinity College in Cambridge, England. It was while he was at Cambridge that he developed his **Three Laws of Motion**, the monumental achievement of a young life that had already experienced several major milestones. The Three Laws included the following:

Isaac Newton

1. *Inertia:* A body, if left to itself and free of action of other bodies, will remain at rest if it is at rest, or it will continue to move at a constant velocity if it is in motion.
2. *Motion:* The rate of change of the momentum of a body measures, in direction and magnitude, the force acting on it.
3. *Action/Reaction:* For every action there is an equal and opposite reaction.

In 1687, he published his *Mathematical Principles of Natural Philosophy.* In this work known universally as the *Principia* (because it was written and originally published in Latin), Newton demonstrated the structure of the universe, explained the movement of the planets, and calculated the mass of the sun, the planets, and their moons. Where Columbus and Magellan had proven that the earth was spherical, Newton proved that the earth is *not* a perfect sphere but rather an *oblate spheroid*—slightly flattened at the poles by the centrifugal force of its rotation.

Just as Marco Polo and Columbus expanded our ancestors' view of the geographical parameters of the world, Newton did more than anyone before (or since, until **Albert Einstein**) to help people understand the physical forces that govern all matter, from the stars in the sky to the apples on a backyard tree. The *Principia* was so complex that only serious scientists could understand it, but when they did, they agreed with the great English poet **Alexander Pope (1688–1744)** who wrote:

Nature and Nature's laws lay hid in night:
God said, Let Newton be! and all was light.

THE RIGHTS of citizens in relation to their kings and rulers have varied through the centuries. The Greeks instituted a form of democracy in which the rights of citizens were broad, but most rulers governed with the belief that their word was law. This changed somewhat in England when King John signed the Magna Carta in 1215. The Magna Carta stated, "no free man shall be taken or imprisoned except by the lawful judgment of his peers and by the law of the land." The underlying principle of this statement is known as **habeas corpus**, which is Latin for "you shall have the body"; in other words, a person cannot be held in jail or against his will without evidence of wrongdoing.

In 1628, **Charles I of England (1600–1649)** declared martial law and used the principle of the **Divine Right of Kings** to jail members of the opposition. Their lawyers swore out writs of habeas corpus, but the jailer told them that the men were being held by special command of the king. The judge upheld the king on the grounds that he *was* the law. The authoritarian Charles I was deposed in 1649, and the monarchy was abolished. Yet it was not until 1679, long after the restoration of the monarchy in 1660, that Parliament compelled Charles II to accept habeas corpus as a specific statute.

Today, the legal systems of most of the world's democratic nations support the principle of habeas corpus. The Constitution of the United States declares that the "privilege of the writ of habeas corpus shall not be suspended, unless, when in cases of rebellion or invasion, the public safety may require it." The privilege was suspended by President Lincoln during the Civil War. At first, Congress did not sanction this, but in 1863, Congress voted to give the president that power.

The trial of Charles I

Habeas corpus is one of the most fundamental principles of the criminal justice system. It guides the actions of police and prosecutors even though it is not specifically invoked.

IN THE two centuries after Columbus opened Europe's eyes to the existence of the Western Hemisphere, the great powers established their dominions. The Spanish took control of everything south of what is now the United States, except Brazil, which came under Portuguese rule. The English claimed the eastern part of what is now the United States, and the French dominated all the land to the north and west of the English.

Beavers were plentiful in the area around the Great Lakes and the St. Lawrence River, and the French discovered that their fur was of a high quality. Soon a great deal of conflict developed between the English and French over the burgeoning fur trade.

In 1670, **King Charles II (1630–1685)** chartered the **Hudson Bay Company**, which marked the beginning of a major British effort to exploit the resources of the territory north of the St. Lawrence River.

In 1756, the **Seven Years' War** in Europe pitted England and Prussia against France and her allies Austria, Russia, Saxony, Sweden, and later Spain. The war involved British and French interests in North America as a sort of sideshow but one that ultimately would have much more far-reaching results than the clash in Europe.

King George II sent the young but brilliant **General James Wolfe (1727–1759)** to command the English forces against the French **General Marquis Louis-Joseph de Montcalm (1712–1759)**. The climax of Wolfe's campaign was the battle for control of the French city of **Quebec**. The English succeeded in sealing off the St. Lawrence River to prevent supplies from coming into Quebec, but Montcalm remained confident that the heavily fortified city was impregnable. The fortifications, after all, thwarted English attacks in 1690 and 1716. The English surprised the French by scaling the high

General James Wolfe

cliffs west of Quebec and overwhelmed the defenders. Wolfe was killed in the assault, but his plan worked. His forces were able to seize the capital of French Canada. Montcalm was also killed, making the contest unique in that both commanding generals died while leading their troops in battle.

The French defeat at Quebec assured England superpower status and gave it unquestioned supremacy over most of North America already settled by Europeans. This predominance was destined to be short-lived, however, as unrest was already brewing in the thirteen colonies to the south of the St. Lawrence River.

Captain James Cook

BRITISH SEA captain **James Cook (1728–1779)** was the last of the great navigators of the discovery epoch that began with Columbus. He surveyed more area of the earth than anyone before him, and claimed Australia and New Zealand for England.

During his four years in the Royal Navy, Cook proved to be a navigational genius. In 1768, he was given command of an expedition taking English astronomers to view a transit of Venus from the South Pacific, after which he was to explore the region for the crown. Cook visited **New Zealand**, became the first to chart its entire coastline, visited **New Guinea**, and, in 1770, he claimed the East Coast of **Australia** under the name **New South Wales**. On his first voyage, Cook had explored more territory than any other explorer had.

In 1772, Cook set out again, becoming the first man to map the coastline of **Antarctica**. On his third voyage in 1776, he discovered the **Hawaiian Islands** (which he named the **Sandwich Islands**), explored the North American coast from Oregon to Alaska, and sailed through the Bering Strait into the Arctic Ocean. It was in 1779, during this third voyage, that he was stabbed to death in Hawaii.

Cook's greatest legacy lies in the settlement of Australia and New Zealand, which had begun before his death, and in having been the first man to explore all the myriad lands within, and on the rim of, the world's largest ocean.

◆ **ALTHOUGH THE** Industrial Revolution was probably inevitable, it is still considered one of the events in human history that truly altered its course. The Industrial Revolution was an amalgam of ideas about machines and their potential for expanding the physical power of humankind, whether it was the power to manufacture goods or the power to move quickly over the surface of the earth.

The first spark of the Industrial Revolution occurred in England with the mechanization of the textile industry. Activities that had previously been done in home workshops were moved to larger, more efficient factories thanks to the spinning machines invented by **Sir Richard Arkwright (1732–1792)** and **James Hargraves (?–1778)**. While there was no shortage of ideas and new machines at the dawn of the Industrial Revolution, few would have been possible without the one machine that subsequently provided the power for the others: the **steam engine**.

The first practical steam engine—one that could not only run itself but also run another machine as well—was the brainchild of Scottish inventor **James Watt (1736–1819)**. Watt studied earlier attempts to build steam engines and made numerous changes, including adding insulation to prevent heat loss and converting the vertical thrust of the steam piston to the circular motion of a drive shaft. His first steam engine was completed in 1769. Soon after, Watt's invention was quickly put into use to automate factory equipment, such as lathes and spinning machines. The Industrial Revolution had begun.

By the early nineteenth century, large-scale applications of steam power, such as locomotives and steamships, made their appearance. **Richard Trevithick (1771–1833)**, a British mechanical engineer, built the first practical steam locomotive in 1802, while an American, **Robert Fulton (1765–1815)**,

James Watt's steam engine

constructed the first practical steamship in 1807. By the 1830s, there were steam railways in service in both England and the United States, and steamships were routinely crossing the Atlantic Ocean.

England was the first nation to embrace the Industrial Revolution due in part to ample supplies of coal to fuel the steam engines that powered the industry. But by the 1860s, France, Germany, and most of northern Europe also became industrialized. The United States embraced the Industrial Revolution early in the nineteenth century, but full industrialization was hampered by distance. When this was overcome by the development of a cross-country railroad network, the new nation across the Atlantic would surpass England as an industrial power. From that moment until the present day, industrial power became the primary measure of national importance. From the United States in the 1920s–1960s to Germany and Japan in the 1980s, political prominence followed economic success.

ENGLAND'S FIRST settlement in North America was established at Jamestown, Virginia, in 1607. It was a tenuous foothold in an untamed wilderness. Over the next 150 years, other settlements sprang up, flourished, and eventually grew into cities that rivaled many in Europe for their comfort and sophistication.

After several generations had been born in England's thirteen colonies, there was an increasing number of people living in these American cities who spoke English and paid

The signing of the Declaration of Independence

English taxes but had never seen England. Moreover, many had parents and grandparents who had never been to England. In fact, most people had come to think of themselves not as English but as American.

From his perspective in England, **King George III** viewed the Americans simply as Englishmen living abroad and thus liable for British taxes. However, since they were not living *in* England, they were not represented in Parliament. To Americans, this became an unacceptable situation, and the cry of "no taxation without representation" rang out. The British sent troops to their rebellious colonies, and the two sides came to blows on April 19, 1775, when an American militia met the British at the **Battle of Lexington and Concord**. This confrontation marked the beginning of what was to be a five-and-a-half-year-long **American Revolutionary War**.

The American colonists were at war with the only national government they had ever known. The thirteen individual colonial governments then decided to work together under the auspices of a single **Continental Congress**.

On July 4, 1776, fifty-six colonial representatives of Connecticut, Delaware, Georgia, Maryland, Massachusetts, New Hampshire, New Jersey, New York, North Carolina, Pennsylvania, Rhode Island, South Carolina, and Virginia met in Philadelphia to sign their **Declaration of Independence**. "When in the course of human events, it becomes necessary for one people to dissolve the political bands which have connected them with another, and to assume among the powers of the earth, the separate and equal station to which the Laws of Nature and of Nature's God entitle them, a decent respect to the opinions of mankind requires that they should declare the causes which impel them to the separation. We hold these truths to be self-evident, that all men are created equal, that they are endowed by their Creator with certain unalienable Rights, that among these are Life, Liberty and the Pursuit of Happiness."

Having declared independence, the new nation had to fight Britain to achieve that status. The Revolutionary War was long and difficult. The decisive battle occurred when **General George Washington (1732–1799)** defeated the British Army under **General Charles Cornwallis (1738–1805)** at Yorktown, Virginia, in 1781. In 1787, the new nation adopted its Constitution and George Washington became its first president.

FOR CENTURIES, the world's political history had been filled with countless instances of would-be kings overthrowing, or plotting to overthrow, reigning monarchs and kingdoms. In the late eighteenth century, a new phenomenon began to occur. Common people began to rise up in opposition to the monarchies that ruled them, and they won. More than just isolated instances involving minor territories, these were important revolutions in major countries, like England and France.

The storming of the Bastille, July 14, 1789

First, England's chief colonial possession in North America declared itself independent and emerged as a new nation. Next, the French people, weary of the absolute despotism of the kings of the **House of Bourbon**, rebelled against **Louis XVI (1754–1793)**, who had been in power since 1774 as the fifth of the Bourbon monarchs. Both the middle class and the poor had long been unhappy with the power and privileges of the nobility, but the catalyst that ignited their revolutionary anger came when Louis declared the nobility exempt from taxes.

On July 14, 1789, an enormous throng of people stormed and captured the **Bastille**, the royal fortress in Paris. Louis XVI, who at the time was in residence at his **Versailles** palace, was both stunned and powerless as the people declared themselves to be citizens of France and no longer subjects of the king. Louis XVI had been so out of touch with reality that he had no idea of the depth of discontent his countrymen felt. His queen, the Austrian-born **Marie Antoinette (1755–1793)** was equally naive. When told that people were angry because they had no bread to eat, she remarked, "Let them eat cake!"

As the momentum of the revolution grew, anarchy reigned in France, especially Paris. The king, the queen, and their family were placed under house arrest and later imprisoned. Finally, in the winter of 1792–1793, they were beheaded one by one on the guillotine.

Monarchs in the surrounding countries of Austria, Prussia, and England threatened to invade the fledgling republic, which was ruled by a committee known as the **National Convention**, and Prussia finally launched an attack. The French Republic not only beat back the Prussians but also counterattacked into the Netherlands and occupied **Savoy**. Back home, however, the central coalition that had overthrown the king began to fall apart. The National Convention was replaced by another committee known as the **Directoire** in 1795, but this mechanism failed to create a truly democratic republic.

In 1799, the **First Republic of France** failed. Although it would not be reinstated until 1848 and would not return permanently until 1871, the absolute monarchy of the Bourbons was gone forever. The seeds of reform that would eventually topple all absolute monarchies in Europe had been sown.

FROM THE time of the Magna Carta to the time of the American Declaration of Independence, the issues of personal freedom, voting rights, and individual liberty had been major points of conflict in the nations of Europe and eventually North America. Gradually, the power of kings and queens was compromised, and the rights of common people were being recognized. England established a constitutional monarchy with an elected Parliament, and by the end of the eighteenth century, both the United States and France stood as independent republics. Democracy seemed to be on the rise. Men had been given the right to vote, and they were using it.

Mary Wollstonecraft

At the time, all of the hard-won democratic rights that were being granted were enjoyed only by men. It was as though women did not matter, or worse, that they were simply men's property. Conventional theory in Europe—and indeed in much of the world—held that "a woman's place was in the home" and not in the halls of public life or where public policy was ratified.

A growing awareness of the inequity of women's legal inequality to men occurred somewhere before the end of the eighteenth century. In 1789 in France, **Olympe de Gouges (1748–1793)** published *Declaration of the Rights of Woman*, a reaction to what she considered an obvious omission from the French Revolutionists' *Declaration of the Rights of Man*. A petition for women's suffrage presented to the French National Assembly that same year was refused, and in fact, the code of laws, promulgated under Napoleon, deprived French women of many rights they had formerly enjoyed.

At the same time, an English governess, **Mary Wollstonecraft (1759–1797)**, was inspired by the French Revolution and Olympe de Gouges's protest, and published *A Vindication of the Rights of Women,* which has remained a landmark text in the women's rights movement. Wollstonecraft believed that girls and women should be permitted equal access to education, that they should be allowed to hold jobs other than as maids and governesses, and that they should be allowed to become doctors and own their own businesses. Women's rights, having long been denied, became a burning issue, one that would not go away.

Progress was slow in the nineteenth century, although women were given greater access to education. In America, **Susan B. Anthony (1820–1906)** was a leader in the antislavery and women's suffrage movements. It was not until the twentieth century, however, that women were able to exercise one of the most basic rights of a democratic society: the right to vote. Australian women gained the right in 1902, English women in 1918, and American women, through the **Nineteenth Amendment** to the United States Constitution, on August 26, 1920, although the Territory of Wyoming had passed a women's suffrage law in 1869. French women were finally given the right to vote in 1945.

FROM THE time of the Caesars to the time of Hitler, there was no one, not even the Holy Roman emperors, who dominated Europe as completely as **Napoleon Bonaparte (1769–1821)**.

For ten years between 1789 and 1799, France was essentially ruled by anarchy or by committee. During this time, Napoleon was a rapidly rising young general in the French Republic army, and he became the first powerful political figure to arise in France after the confusion that followed the revolution. Napoleon, who had won a series of brilliant victories against the Austrians in Italy, invaded Egypt in 1798 and marched into Cairo and then into Jerusalem. These events greatly inspired the French public, and when Napoleon returned to France in 1799, he was acknowledged as a national hero.

Meanwhile, France had been without a single leader for a decade, and the weak, ineffective **Directoire**, which ruled the country, was on the verge of collapse. Napoleon was the natural choice to lead the country. In November 1799, the Directoire was replaced by a **Consulate** with Napoleon as first consul. Although he was now the master of France, he continued to dream of an empire on the scale of Charlemagne's.

Napoleon served as first consul until 1804. Due to his immense popularity, the French people, who had thrown out the Bourbon kings in 1792, allowed him to transform the Consulate into an empire. Napoleon invited the pope to crown him the French emperor at Notre Dame Cathedral in Paris on May 18, 1804. However, when the climactic moment came, Napoleon lifted the crown from the pope's hands and crowned himself.

Immediately, Napoleon began building a **French Empire**. He already controlled France, the Netherlands, and Italy but was opposed by Austria, England, Russia, and Prussia. He planned an invasion of England, which he was forced to call off, but when he faced the Russian and Austrian armies at **Austerlitz** in December 1805, his brilliant tactics carried the day. Napoleon went on to win an incredible string of victories that included defeating the Prussians at **Jena** in 1806 and the Austrians at **Friedland** in 1807. By this time, Napoleon had accomplished his goal of effectively controlling an area of Europe even larger than Charlemagne's empire. He now dominated France, Poland, Italy, and everything in between, including Austria and all the German states of the old Holy Roman Empire.

Britain remained his archenemy. Although Napoleon was able to cut off most of Britain's trade with continental Europe, he was never able to completely stop it. In 1810, when the Russians refused to join his blockade, he decided to invade Russia. He managed to capture Moscow in September 1812, but after severe winter weather threatened his supply lines, he was forced to retreat. This military disaster was the beginning of the end of Napoleon's reign of power. His allies and the states that composed his domain began to revolt. He was forced to withdraw from Austria and Germany, and his empire collapsed. On April 11, 1814, he abdicated and was forced into exile on the island of Elba. The man who had once ruled most of Europe was now forced to be a tenant on a tiny, rocky island.

However, Napoleon's greatest contribution was his **Napoleonic Code**, a modern structure of civil laws that remains the basis for French law to this day.

AFTER MORE than a decade of glory, the collapse of the French Empire and the departure of Napoleon in 1814 left France in a state of total chaos not unlike that which it had experienced during the revolution. Amazingly, at this point, the Bourbon monarchy was restored, but Louis XVIII ruled for only ten months.

Napoleon grew restless during his exile and returned to France. He was welcomed in Paris with open arms, mostly for nostalgic reasons since he represented France's glorious past. For a brief one hundred days from March 10, 1815, the clock seemed to have been turned back a decade.

A large British, Prussian, and Dutch force fought Napoleon's army at Waterloo

However, his old rivals, especially the British, were not at all pleased that he was back on the throne. Napoleon knew that he would soon be attacked and that he had to move quickly if he was to restore his empire. He had to gamble that a fast victory would bring the states of Europe toppling down like a line of dominoes.

A large British, Prussian, and Dutch force, under the command of the Prussian general **Gebhard Leberecht von Blücher (1742–1819)** and **Arthur Wellesley (1769–1852), the Duke of Wellington**, had been gathered in Belgium. At first, things went well for Napoleon. His large and superbly equipped force drove a wedge between Blücher and Wellington, and defeated the Prussians at **Ligny** on June 16. The British retreated to a little crossroads village called **Waterloo**, where Napoleon caught up with them on June 17. Napoleon prepared to attack Wellington on June 18, but rain from the night before made it difficult to move his canons into position.

Napoleon finally attacked at 11 a.m., and the battle raged for ten hours. Blücher's remaining force joined Wellington in the late afternoon, which helped to turn the tide. By the morning of June 19, the French had been defeated and 50,000 men lay dead and dying. Napoleon himself retreated to Paris, where he abdicated, for the second time, four days later. He surrendered to the British and was taken to the island of St. Helena in the South Atlantic, where he lived until he died from cancer on May 8, 1821.

Waterloo was one of the major turning points in European history because if Napoleon had won, he stood a good chance of reestablishing his empire and once again making France the dominant power in Europe—and possibly the world—for the rest of the nineteenth century.

As it was, France would never regain the power and influence that it had enjoyed under Napoleon. He had lost the French Empire in Europe, and he had sold an even larger area—**Louisiana**—in North America to the United States. Waterloo marked the beginning of *Pax Britannica*, a period of more than a century during which Britain reigned as the world's leading superpower.

FOR CENTURIES, humankind recorded images of reality with pen and brush. Ancient peoples drew pictures of the animals they hunted. In China and in Renaissance Europe, the painter's art became "fine" art as the artist captured not only perfect likenesses but a sense of drama and motion.

In the meantime, many people shared the dream of being able to preserve an image directly and immediately by mechanical means. The realization of this dream would be more than a scientific achievement; it would mark a turning point in the way we perceive our own as well as others' environment.

The dream had its roots in the principle of the **camera obscura**, in which sunlight reflected from an object and directed through a small hole into a dark room or box, will project an inverted image of the object onto the opposite wall. In 1717, German doctor J. H. Schulze discovered that light darkened silver chloride, and in 1824, **Joseph Nicéphore Niépce (1765–1833)** discovered that a sun-printed image could be permanently fixed by coating a metal plate with bitumen before placing it in a camera obscura for a prolonged exposure. The resulting picture was called a **heliotype**. In 1829, Niépce entered into a partnership with **Louis-Jacques Daguerre (1787–1851)** to perfect this method. In 1839, Daguerre unveiled the **daguerreotype** process. In 1879, **George Eastman (1854–1932)** of Rochester, New York, invented an emulsion-coating machine that allowed him to manufacture photographic plates in large quantities. In 1889, Eastman began marketing strips of celluloid with emulsion on them that could be used to make a series of photographic negatives. The idea of a "roll of film" cranked through a camera was the basis for popular photography, which eventually paved the way for motion pictures.

While Eastman's development made motion pictures possible, the underlying phenomenon, known as the persistence of vision, was understood by **Leonardo da Vinci (1452–1519)** as early as the fifteenth century. In the nineteenth century, inventors produced various handheld devices in which one could view images arranged on a spinning wheel or disk that appeared to move. In 1889, **William Friese-Greene (1855–1921)** in England and **Thomas Alva Edison (1847–1931)** in the United States decided to print multiple images on transparent film that could be projected.

Edison adapted this for use in his **kinetograph**, which was the first camera specifically designed to film motion pictures, and his **kinetoscope**, which was the first motion picture projector. Both were patented in 1891, and the kinetoscope had its debut in New York as a peep-show device in 1893. Edison had failed to patent his inventions abroad, so it was possible for two brothers in France named **Auguste (1862–1954)** and **Louis Lumière (1864–1948)** to build what amounted to an improved version of Edison's **kinetograph**, which they called **Cinématographe**. The first large, full-scale projection of motion pictures on a theater wall took place at the Grand Café in Paris on March 22, 1895. Edison went on to further refine his process, producing his own projector, the **vitascope**, which led to the first projection of a motion picture in a theater in the United States at Koster and Bial's Music Hall in New York City on April 23, 1896.

The impact of photography on all aspects of modern culture and commerce has been significant. Imagine how different modern mass communications would be without photographic images or motion pictures.

BY THE nineteenth century, as the steam engine boosted the speed and distance capabilities of vehicles on both land and sea, a clear need emerged for a means of instantaneous communication over long distances. It became critical to quickly communicate with places that were too far away to be seen, just to keep ahead of the faster ships and trains. In 1791, **Abbe Claude Chappe (1763–1805)** coined the term **optical telegraph** to describe his use of a series of towers to relay a message that was visible by one tower from the one before it. Chappe's system involved a string of 120 towers that could convey a message between Paris and the Mediterranean in less than an hour, which was far less time than the fastest horse and rider.

A nineteenth-century telegraph office

All of these systems depended on visible signals. **Telegraphy** was a major breakthrough in communications because it made instant communication possible between two people who were out of sight of each other. The idea of sending coded messages by means of electricity dates back to the early eighteenth century. **Georges-Louis Lesage (1724–1803)** in Switzerland in 1774 developed a machine that transmitted signals by means of a separate wire dedicated to each letter of the alphabet. His system was based on the writings of a mysterious Scottish inventor known only as "C.M.," which had been published in 1753.

After Lesage, there were many efforts to refine the telegraph. These were carried out by Chappe in France, **Carl Friedrich Gauss (1777–1855)** and **Wilhelm Eduard Weber (1804–1891)** in Germany and **Alessandro Volta (1745–1827)** in Italy. Based on the tests carried out by these men, several experimental telegraph lines were set up.

However, the first practical telegraph system was developed by the American inventor **Samuel F. B. Morse (1791–1872)**. Morse also devised the **Morse Code**, which consisted of a series of taps of the key that made electrical contact. Thus, each letter of the alphabet consisted of short taps (dots) combined with longer contacts (dashes), and this system became the universal language of the telegraph.

Morse first demonstrated his telegraph to President Martin Van Buren on February 21, 1838, and by 1843 a workable commercial telegraph line was in place between Washington and Baltimore. Within the next two years, most major American and European cities were connected by telegraph, and in the 1850s, England and Sweden were linked to continental Europe by means of underwater cables. Europe and America were joined by an underwater cable between Newfoundland and Ireland in 1858, and Queen Victoria sent a ninety-word message to President James Buchanan.

The advent of instantaneous long distance communications revolutionized the way people viewed time and distance. After 1838, the perceived size of the world of world grew progressively smaller as people became able to transmit information over great distances more quickly than before.

IN ONE of history's rare twists of coincidence, the conditions in virtually every country in continental Europe reached the flashpoint of revolution in 1848.

Prior to 1848, England had already undergone dramatic changes. During the 1640s, England had been wracked by civil war, which had led to the overthrow of **Charles I (1600–1649)** in 1649 and the establishment of **Oliver Cromwell (1599–1658)** as Protector. In 1660, two years after Cromwell's death, under **Charles II (1630–1685)**, a constitutional monarchy was in place.

Prince Klemens Wenzel von Metternich meeting with Napoleon

In France, the revolution of 1789 that overturned the monarchy initially led to chaos, then to Napoleon in 1799, and back again to the monarchy in 1815. By 1848, however, France, like Italy, Austria, and the German states, was once again on the verge of revolt.

After the chaotic years of the Napoleonic Wars and French expansionism, the other great powers of Europe—Austria, Britain, Prussia, and Russia—joined forces to form a brotherhood of monarchs known as the **Holy Alliance**. This idea originated at the **Congress of Vienna**, held in 1815 under the leadership of Austrian chancellor **Prince Klemens Wenzel von Metternich (1773–1859)**. Indeed, Metternich's brilliant political skills eventually put Austria on Europe's center stage and resulted in the next three decades becoming known as the **"Age of Metternich."**

The members of the Holy Alliance also formed a military coalition called the **Grand Alliance**, to which France was admitted in 1818. The objective of both these unions was to preserve peace and order in Europe by preventing any Alliance member from becoming stronger than another and by pledging to maintain orderly, hereditary monarchies in all member states. However, at this time, the Industrial Revolution began to create major changes in the fabric of European society. The people whom the monarchs ruled were no longer merely rural peasants but factory workers, professional people, and business owners. This new breed of citizenry resented being treated like serfs by a class of hereditary nobles.

The revolution started in Paris on February 23, 1848. The monarchy collapsed, and by December **Louis Napoleon (1808–1873)** organized a plebiscite and declared himself president of a Second Republic in France. Soon the cities of the Austrian-dominated, but still disunited, Italian states were also seething. Unification under a republic was seen as a desirable objective.

Simultaneously, Vienna, choked with immigrants from throughout the Austrian Empire, erupted, and Metternich himself was forced to flee to England. **Ferdinand II (1810–1859)** tentatively granted rights to his subjects, but the revolution continued to spread to all parts of his empire as well as to Prussia and the German states. Ferdinand was compelled to abdicate in favor of his son Franz Josef I. The shockwaves that emanated from the 1848 revolutions were tremendous. Except for Louis Napoleon declaring himself emperor in 1852, France would never again be ruled by a monarch. Elsewhere in Europe, the Age of Metternich had also crumbled. Though many of the continent's great monarchies would survive until 1918, their days were numbered.

IT WAS the chance discovery of a yellow pebble by a man named **James W. Marshall (1810–1885)** that began the greatest mass migration in modern history. Except for the Civil War, it was the event that would most define the United States in the nineteenth century.

For the first several decades of its existence, the United States essentially consisted of the original thirteen colonies plus adjacent lands in the wilderness of Appalachia and northwest of the Great Lakes

A family of "forty-niners" travel west in their covered wagon

country. Although the size of the nation had nearly doubled in 1803 with the purchase of Louisiana from France, most of this territory was a vast, uncharted area known as the Great American Desert. Farther west, Spain and (after 1821) Mexico controlled the areas which are now California and the states of the Southwest. However, Mexico's control of California became more and more tenuous as a steady trickle of American settlers continued into both Oregon and California. In 1846, the Americans declared a **"California Republic,"** the same year the United States purchased Oregon from Britain and declared war on Mexico. Two years later, in 1848, Mexico ceded California, along with present-day Nevada, Utah, Colorado, Arizona, and New Mexico, to the United States. By that time, the American population of the region had grown far greater than the Mexican population.

Still, California remained a long, grueling journey from "civilization." However, this would all soon change. On January 24,

1848, James W. Marshall, a carpenter at **John Sutter's mill** near Sacramento in California's Sierra Nevada foothills, discovered an unusually large gold nugget. A further search turned up more nuggets, and soon the phrase "there's gold in them thar' hills" echoed throughout central California.

By 1849, the news of the gold strike had reached the East Coast, and the **California Gold Rush** was on. Over 50,000 **"forty-niners"** streamed into California, arriving by land and by ship around the tip of South America. Many nuggets weighing nearly one hundred pounds were discovered. The total quantity of gold dug out of the Sierra in the first five years alone of the gold rush was valued at more than the rest of the world's total production.

San Francisco, as the gateway to the gold fields, continued to grow in importance, and its harbor became known as the "Golden Gate." The city's population grew from 800 to 25,000 in the space of a few months, and by the time California was admitted to the Union in 1850, the state's population was more than double what it had been when gold was first discovered at Sutter's Mill. The financial ripples emanating from the gold rush profoundly affected money markets all over the world. The mass migration of people precipitated by the gold rush forever altered the course of American history by creating, almost overnight, an American civilization on the West Coast of the continent.

THROUGHOUT HISTORY, numerous attempts have been made to determine exactly when the world actually began. Prior to the twentieth century, modern dating techniques were not available, so Western scholars depended on a literal reading of the Bible, which, of course, begins with a description in the Book of Genesis of the creation of the world. By working backward from the birth of Jesus Christ (then calculated at the year zero), scholars counted all references to spans of time and determined that the world had been created in 4004 BCE. Today, most people accept the idea that the world occurred 4.5 billion years ago and is part of an **evolutionary process**. People who subscribe to this theory are known as **evolutionists**. People who believe the Bible to be the literal truth are known as **creationists**.

The concepts of **creationism** and **evolutionism** are at odds with each other, not over the issue of whether or when the world was created but over the issue of when and how everything else was created. Creationists believe that all species—from oysters to humans—were created in the exact same form as we know them today and that they have always had the same form. Evolutionists believe that a species is capable of changing from generation to generation and that two similar yet distinct species—such as lions and tigers—may have had a common ancestor millions of years ago. This latter idea, which seems a commonplace one today, may have been suggested in Greece as early as the fifth century BCE, but in the nineteenth century, a fully developed theory of evolution was still unheard of, and certainly no one

The theorized stages of human evolution

had been able to work out the details of such a theory.

The first person to formulate a detailed theory of evolution was a young Englishman named **Charles Robert Darwin (1809–1882)**. An average student in school, Darwin had just graduated from Cambridge when he accepted an opportunity to serve as an unpaid naturalist on a five-year survey expedition being undertaken by the vessel **HMS Beagle**. The Beagle left England in December 1831 and returned in October 1836. During the long voyage, the ship's crew surveyed South America, Australia, New Zealand, and countless islands en route.

It was while on this journey that the energetic Darwin began to synthesize his theory of evolution. He discovered that, on remote islands such as the Galapagos, species were remarkably different from related species on the mainland. This led him to the realization that while they did have common ancestors, over the course of time, their dissimilar environments had caused them to evolve differently. He continued to refine his theory of **natural selection**, which stated that species evolved because nature "selected" those plants and animals best suited to specific environments. It took Darwin over twenty years to completely formulate his theory, but when his book *On the Origin of Species* finally appeared in 1859, it radically impacted the course and theory of biological science by changing people's perspective of world history and the environment in which they lived.

WHEN THE United States was formed, it was just that: a group of nominally united states. The original concept was for these individual states to have extensive powers of self-government over their own affairs, while a national government would concern itself with foreign policy, a common currency, and a common postal system. As these individual states evolved, different social and economic systems emerged. The Northern states enthusiastically embraced the Industrial Revolution, while the Southern states remained largely agricultural. **Slavery**, which involved the importation of Africans against their will to work as farm laborers, had been outlawed in the seven Northern states in 1804. However, it remained an integral part of life in the South, where massive cotton fields were the region's economic backbone.

President Abraham Lincoln

By the 1840s, slavery had become the most divisive political issue in the United States. A powerful movement in the North sought the abolition of slavery, which the South strongly resisted. For the **abolitionists**, it was a moral issue. They believed that slavery was simply wrong. For Southerners, most of whom did not actually own slaves, it was solely an issue of **states' rights**—the right of individual states to govern their own internal affairs as guaranteed in the Constitution. The slavery issue was further complicated by the question of whether new states admitted to the Union ought to be slave states or free states. For example, the two largest states admitted up to that time were split. Texas had entered as a slave state in 1845 and California as a free state in 1850.

By the late 1850s, the Southern states had begun to openly discuss the possibility of seceding from the United States and forming a separate nation. The disagreement came to a head during the 1860 presidential campaign. The Republican Party candidate, **Abraham Lincoln (1809–1865)** of Illinois, strongly favored abolition, but his primary concern was to preserve the Union. After he was elected, the Southern states quickly moved to secede from the Union even before his inauguration. On February 4, 1861, Alabama, Florida, Georgia, Louisiana, Mississippi, and Texas met in Montgomery, Alabama, to form the **Confederate States of America**, adopting a constitution similar to the U.S. Constitution except for the sanction of slavery. Arkansas, North Carolina, South Carolina, Tennessee, and Virginia also joined the Confederacy, and later Richmond, Virginia (just a day's ride from Washington, DC), was designated the Confederate capital.

Lincoln vowed to go to war to restore the Union, but the Confederacy initiated the first battle when they attacked the United States Army post at **Fort Sumter** on April 12, 1861. A war of national preservation had begun involving two profoundly different views of how one nation—or two separate nations—should be preserved.

WHEN THE eleven Southern states declared themselves to be the independent **Confederate States of America** on February 4, 1861, it was a disastrous blow for the unity of the United States and for those who wished to see the Union preserved, such as President Abraham Lincoln. However, there was also a belief in the North that prompt military action would quickly bring the Confederacy to its knees.

In both total population and armed fighting strength, the North overshadowed the South three to one, and the North's manufacturing and industrial strength had nine times the capacity of the South's. Despite this, the first major armed clash at **Bull Run** on July 21, 1861, was an overwhelming Confederate victory that clearly showed that the **American Civil War** would be neither short nor easy.

Over the next two years, the Union forces attempted to go on the offensive, but Confederate general **Robert Edward Lee (1807–1870)** consistently outmaneuvered them. Lee constantly threatened to capture Washington, DC, while the Union troops failed to get even within striking distance of Richmond.

Lee's brilliance as a commander and a tactician, combined with Lincoln's inability to find a fully competent Union Army commander, led to a string of stunning Confederate victories.

Meanwhile, the Union Navy blockaded the Confederate ports, and the North's massive industrial machine was able to replace Union material losses quickly. The Confederate armies were courageous and well led, but they began to become weary as the war dragged on.

The tide of the American Civil War turned in July 1863 in what are remembered as two of the conflict's bloodiest confrontations.

Lee's forces, attempting to invade the North, were stopped at **Gettysburg, Pennsylvania**, and Union general **Ulysses Simpson Grant (1822–1885)** captured the Confederate stronghold at **Vicksburg, Mississippi**, on the Mississippi River.

Grant followed his success at Vicksburg by defeating the Confederate forces at **Chattanooga, Tennessee**, on November 25, 1863. It appeared that Lincoln had finally found a general who could match Lee, and who hopefully could bring the war to a successful close.

In the final phase of the war, Grant pushed south from Washington and **General William Tecumseh Sherman (1820–1891)** cut a swath through the heart of the Confederacy. Sherman seized control of Atlanta on September 2, 1864, and Savannah on December 20. He then turned back north. Richmond now lay in a vice grip between Grant and Sherman.

Lee finally surrendered to Grant on April 9, 1865, at the **Appomattox Courthouse** in Virginia.

The Civil War was the greatest domestic disaster in American history. Union forces lost 364,511 troops and the Confederates lost 133,821. In fact, more Americans died in the Civil War than in any other war, including World War II. Slavery in America was abolished forever, and Abraham Lincoln's dream of a united country was at last secured.

Unfortunately, Lincoln himself did not live to enjoy the fruits of his hard-won peace. He was assassinated by an unemployed actor and Confederate sympathizer named **John Wilkes Booth (1838–1865)** at Ford's Theater in Washington, DC, on April 15, 1865.

IN THE middle of the nineteenth century, Japan was still a feudal monarchy whose social structure had changed little in centuries. It had been ruled since 660 BCE by a succession of emperors who called themselves *tenshi*—"the sons of heaven." Being an island nation, Japan was geographically isolated from mainland Asia—and indeed from the rest of the world—completely removed from the mainstream of world history, and this was exactly how the emperors preferred it. Japanese society was very rigid, and immigration was nonexistent. In fact, the edict of 1635 forbade the Japanese from leaving their native country. Foreign merchants were strictly prohibited from conducting business in Japan, although after 1842 certain ports began to allow foreign ships to dock for water and supplies.

This condition of total isolation was destined to change. On July 8, 1853, U.S. Navy commodore **Matthew Calbraith Perry (1794–1858)** sailed into **Edo Bay** with a squadron of heavily armed gunboats and a message from **President Millard Fillmore (1800–1874)**: Japan should open its harbors to American trade or risk war. Perry gave Japan the better part of a year to consider this ultimatum, and when he returned, the **Treaty of Kanagawa** was signed on March 31, 1854. Japan had finally joined the world community.

By 1858, the United States, Britain, and France had established supply bases in Japan, but there was a good deal of unrest. It was not until April 6, 1868, that the young **Emperor Mutsuhito (1852–1912)**, also known as **Meiji**, expressly forbade anti-foreign activities and initiated a program to modernize Japan by importing machines and machine tools from the leading edge of the Industrial Revolution. At the time of Perry's first landing at Edo Bay in 1853, Japan was the technological equivalent of Europe in the

Japan isolated itself from the world until 1854

1550s. Within a quarter century of the **Meiji Restoration** of 1868, Japan had industrialized to the technological level of Europe and the United States.

It was an effort that the world had never before witnessed, with the possible exception of Japan's resurrection after the devastation of World War II. Japan would enter the twentieth century as the leading industrial power in Asia.

THE CALIFORNIA Gold Rush of 1848 and the subsequent mass migration of people to the Pacific coast clearly demonstrated the need for a quicker means of transportation across the North American continent. The vast territory between the Mississippi River and the Pacific Ocean was a wilderness that took months to cross. This overland journey was so arduous that many people chose to travel by ship around the tip of South America—a distance nearly eight times as long—rather than chance a crossing by land.

There were numerous proposals for a transcontinental, or Pacific, railroad. For the businessmen of California, who were isolated from the rest of the nation, the need was particularly acute. Routes from Chicago to Puget Sound were considered, as were routes directly across the plains from Omaha to San Francisco. Southern factions promoted the idea of a route through Texas, Arizona, and New Mexico because the weather was generally better than on other proposed routes. But this idea was shelved when the Civil War broke out. Most agreed that the central route was best. The Civil War also underscored the need for a transcontinental railroad, and in 1862 President Abraham Lincoln signed the **Pacific Railroad Act**, which called for the creation of the **Union Pacific Railroad** that would build its lines west from Omaha, Nebraska. Meanwhile, in California, after commissioning a survey to locate the best route across the Sierra Nevada, an independent group of especially enterprising entrepreneurs began work in 1861 on their **Central Pacific Railroad**. Known simply as the "Big Four," they were **Charles Crocker (1822–1888), Mark Hopkins (1802–1887), Collis Huntington (1821–1900),** and **Leland Stanford (1824–1893).**

The Central Pacific was incorporated into the Pacific railroad plan with the idea

The transcontinental railroad made travel across the country much faster

that their track-laying crews would meet on the eastern side of the Sierra Nevada. As the work progressed, it became apparent that the Central Pacific crews worked much more rapidly than initially projected and the Union Pacific crews worked more slowly. It was decided that the two lines would continue construction until they met, wherever they met. The two projects turned into a gigantic race across the open spaces of Nevada, Wyoming, and Utah, with crews laying as much as ten miles of track in a single day!

Finally, on May 10, 1869, locomotives of the two railroads met at **Promontory, Utah,** and a golden spike was driven to mark the joining of the tracks. A journey that once took months could now be accomplished in just a few days. A nation with contiguous states between two oceans was now bound from coast to coast with bands of steel.

TODAY, IT is clearly evident that **Germany** is both the geographic and industrial heart of Europe, but historically, the existence of Germany as a single, unified nation is a relatively recent occurrence. At the time of the Roman Empire, the German tribes remained fiercely independent despite a common language. Even after the tribes were nominally united as part of the **Holy Roman Empire**, which was always ruled by a German figurehead, they persisted as independent states. This largely ceremonial title survived until 1806, the year Napoleon formed a confederation of German states as part of his empire. Ironically, this confederation would eventually constitute the basis for opposition against Napoleon. By the time Napoleon was defeated at Waterloo in 1815, the more than three hundred German states that existed in the Middle Ages had combined into thirty-nine. Among these states were powerful nations, such as Austria and Prussia and other smaller states such as Bavaria and Saxony. However, efforts to unify Germany after the Napoleonic era always resulted in a competition between Prussia and Austria over which would be the dominant entity in a united Germany. Ultimately, Prussia emerged as the most powerful of the German states, and Austria has remained separate from unified Germany ever since, except for the period from 1938 to 1945.

The man most responsible for charting the course of German unification was **Otto Eduard Leopold von Bismarck (1815–1898)**,

Otto von Bismarck

who was appointed as the Prussian envoy to the Bundestag (the diet or council of German states) by **King Friedrich Wilhelm IV (1795–1861)**. He later served as Prussian ambassador to France. This experience provided him with valuable insights that would serve him well. In 1862, Friedrich Wilhelm's brother and heir, **Wilhelm I (1797–1888)**, named Bismarck chancellor of Prussia. Known simply as the **"Iron Chancellor,"** Bismarck went on to serve as the first chancellor of the German Empire from 1871 to 1890. By 1866, Bismarck had engineered a unification of most of the German states under Prussian control. Meanwhile, **Louis Napoleon (1808–1873)** (Emperor Napoleon III after 1852) wanted to extend France's eastern border to the Rhine River and incorporate many German states into the French Empire. On July 19, 1870, Napoleon III declared war on the German states. Thanks to shrewd planning by Bismarck, Prussia was well prepared for attack. The Germans counterattacked, reaching Paris by Christmas Day. The **Franco-Prussian War** ended in a decisive victory, and Prussia now possessed the political power to unite the Germans. On January 18, 1871, the German Empire was proclaimed, with Bismarck as its chancellor.

Bismarck would remain the unquestioned power behind the throne of continental Europe's most powerful monarchy for nearly two decades. Germany itself would remain unified until 1945.

FROM THE time Christopher Columbus first set foot in the Western Hemisphere in 1492, Europeans came in conflict with the native peoples of the Americas. Whereas the Spanish ruthlessly crushed the native empires of Central and South America in the sixteenth century, the conflict in North America was more akin to guerrilla warfare, which persisted on the frontier at the edge of the British colonies.

Official American policy toward the Indians alternated between ignoring them and consciously removing them from specific areas. The **Indian Removal Act** of 1830 called for moving all Native Americans to the land west of the Mississippi River, and in 1837, **Indian Territory** (now the state of Oklahoma) was created as a permanent home for all tribes formerly living in the Southeast section of the United States. This forced relocation served only to postpone the inevitable clash of cultures that would take place as settlers began to cross the plains in growing numbers.

The Plains Indian tribes, such as the Blackfoot, Cheyenne, Crow, and Sioux (Dakota), and the Southwest tribes, such as the Apaches, were primarily nomadic peoples who managed to avoid the Europeans until after the American Civil War. Encounters between the two groups were sporadic, taking place primarily along the immigrant trails. Between 1866 and 1868, however, there were a series of skirmishes in the North Plains known as **Red Cloud's War** (named after the Oglala Sioux chief who was involved). The treaty that ended this conflict guaranteed the Sioux a huge reservation in the Black Hills of the Dakota Territory in exchange for their traditional hunting grounds in the Montana Territory and adjacent lands.

Eight years later, the discovery of gold in the Black Hills brought settlers into the Plains, and warfare again erupted. The Sioux returned to Montana and the U.S. Army forced them to return to their reservation. The army's campaign against the Indians called for a three-pronged pincer attack led by **General George Crook (1828–1890)**, and **Major General John Gibbon** and Brigadier General **Alfred Terry**. Within Terry's command was the flamboyant and young Indian fighter **Colonel George Armstrong Custer (1839–1876)**. Custer, anxious for glory, was eager for his Seventh Cavalry Regiment to be the first to make contact with the Sioux. The Seventh Cavalry was the first to make contact, and Custer attacked immediately. However, over three thousand Sioux and Cheyenne, under the great **Chief Sitting Bull (1831–1890)** of the Hunkpapa Sioux, had gathered on the banks of the Little Bighorn River in what was the largest encampment ever encountered by the U.S. Army in wartime. Custer and his 215-man force were wiped out in forty-five minutes, before the other prongs of the pincer arrived.

The **Battle of the Little Bighorn**, on June 25, 1876, represented the biggest Indian victory. Although the Indians won this battle, they would lose the Indian Wars. The U.S. Army had more soldiers and more potent weapons, so it was preordained that they would ultimately defeat the Native Americans. Within a few years, the Plains tribes were forced onto reservations. By 1886, the last Indians still resisting the U.S. Army, the Apaches led by **Chief Geronimo (1829–1909)** in Arizona, had surrendered. However, the army's terrible defeat in 1876 made clear the fact that the territory of the United States was no longer capable of accommodating both the traditional, nomadic life of the native peoples and the evolution of modern civilization.

PROBABLY NO means of communication has revolutionized the daily lives of ordinary people more than the **telephone**. Simply described, it is a system that converts sound—specifically the human voice—to electrical impulses of various frequencies and then back to sound. In 1831, Englishman **Michael Faraday (1791–1867)** proved that metal vibrations could be converted to electrical impulses. This was the technological basis of the telephone, but no one actually used this system to transmit sound until 1861. That year in Germany, **Philip Reis** is said to have built a simple apparatus that changed sound to electricity and back again to sound. A crude device, it was incapable of transmitting most frequencies, and it was never fully developed.

A practical telephone was actually invented by two men working independently in the United States, Scottish-born **Alexander Graham Bell (1847–1922)** and **Elisha Gray (1835–1901)**. Incredibly, both men filed for a patent on their designs at the New York patent office on February 14, 1876, with Bell beating Gray by only two hours! Although Gray had built the first steel diaphragm/electromagnet receiver in 1874, he wasn't able to master the design of a workable transmitter until after Bell did. Bell had worked tirelessly, experimenting with various types of mechanisms, while Gray had become discouraged.

According to the famous story, the first fully intelligible telephone call occurred on March 6, 1876, when Bell, in one room, called to his assistant in another room. "Come here, Watson," Bell directed. "I want you." Watson heard the request through a receiver connected to the transmitter that Bell had designed. Afterward, he founded the **Bell Telephone Company** (later **AT&T**), which grew to be the largest telephone company in the world.

Alexander Graham Bell (center) makes the first transcontinental telephone call

The first telephone system, known as an exchange, which is a practical communication network between many people who have telephones, was installed in Hartford, Connecticut, in 1877. The first exchange linking two major cities was established between New York and Boston in 1883, and the first exchange outside the United States was built in London in 1879.

◆ **ADVANCES IN** motor power have always been linked to turns in the cultural history of humankind because they expand our ability to affect our environment. It had been James Watt's steam engine—invented in the eighteenth century—that powered the Industrial Revolution of the nineteenth century. It was the invention of the **practical internal combustion engine** that made possible the Industrial Revolution of the twentieth century, with its airplanes, automobiles, lawnmowers, and other engine-driven machines.

There were numerous attempts to build a workable internal combustion engine in the early nineteenth century, but the first successful model was constructed in 1860 by the Belgian-born Frenchman **Étienne Lenoir**. In the meantime, Germans **Nikolaus August Otto (1832–1891)** and **Eugen Langen** invented an "air-breathing" engine in 1867 that greatly improved the fuel efficiency of internal combustion engines. However, the greatest breakthrough, in terms of efficiency and power, was the invention of the four-stroke engine, in which every fourth stroke of the piston was a power (or working) stroke. The four-stroke process was designed in 1862 by Frenchman **Alphonse Beau de Rochas**, but he never built a practical working model. It was Nikolaus Otto who succeeded in building and patenting the first four-stroke internal combustion engine in 1876. In terms of the lives of average people, there is little doubt that the **automobile** is the most revolutionary invention in the history of transportation since the wheel. The basic premise of the automobile is simple: choose a wheeled vehicle from the many types typically pulled by horses or oxen, add a motor and create a self-propelled, personal transportation vehicle. The milestone vehicle was built in Germany in 1889 by **Gottlieb Daimler (1834–1900)**

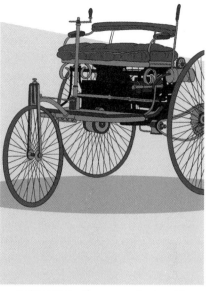

Karl Benz's gasoline-powered automobile

and **Wilhelm Maybach (1846–1929)**. Powered by a 1.5 hp, two-cylinder gasoline engine, it had a four-speed transmission and traveled at 10 mph. Another German, **Karl Benz (1844–1929)**, also built a gasoline-powered car the same year. The gasoline-powered automobile, or motor car, remained largely a curiosity for the rest of the nineteenth century, with only a handful being manufactured in Europe and the United States. The first automobile to be produced in large quantities was the 1901 Oldsmobile, which was built in the United States by **Ransom E. Olds (1864–1950)**, a manufacturer of gasoline engines since 1873. Modern automobile **mass production** and the invention of the modern industrial **assembly line** are credited to **Henry Ford (1863–1947)** of Detroit, Michigan, who built his first gasoline-powered car in 1896. Ford began producing his Model T in 1908, and by 1927, when it was discontinued, over 18 million had rolled off the assembly line.

Guglielmo Marconi with his transmission station

◆ **BOTH THE TELEGRAPH** (1838) and the **telephone** (1875) were enormous leaps forward in the evolution of communication technology. A major limitation of the technology was that the people using them had to be linked by a wire. If the wire was broken, or if a wire could not be run, then communication was impossible.

In 1887, German scientist **Heinrich Hertz (1857–1894)** discovered **radio waves**, but Italian physicist, **Guglielmo Marconi (1874–1937)** first adapted them for use in communication. This milestone occurred in 1895 when he succeeded in transmitting a wireless electronic message over a distance of a mile and a half. In 1898, Eugene Ducretet and Ernest Roger made a wireless transmission across the city of Paris, and on March 28, 1899, Marconi sent the first international wireless message from Dover, England, to Wimereux, France, a distance of thirty-one miles. On December 12, 1901, Marconi successfully conducted the first intercontinental wireless transmission between Poldhu, England, and a receiving station in Newfoundland that was 2,100 miles away.

In 1903, Marconi established a transmission station, designated WCC, in South Wellfleet, Massachusetts. The dedication ceremonies included an exchange of greetings between President Theodore Roosevelt and King Edward VII. In 1904, Marconi entered into an agreement with the Cunard steamship line to create the first ship-to-shore communications system. This system proved to be a vital factor in saving lives in the event of maritime disasters, such as the sinking of the *Titanic*.

DURING THE nineteenth century while the British were building their political and economic empire around the world, the United States' focus was on the economic development of the American territory, an area almost as vast as that of the British Empire. In fact, most European powers—even those as small as Portugal and Belgium—had colonies in Africa and the Far East. By 1898, thanks to a land rich in natural resources and a constantly expanding economy, the United States had become an economic superpower on the world scene. Yet, by European standards, it was not considered a political superpower because it had no colonial empire nor an interest in the subtleties of political developments outside the Western Hemisphere.

Spain, meanwhile, watched its empire in the Western Hemisphere collapse over the course of the nineteenth century as all of the South American republics under their rule won their independence. In 1895, the Cuban people revolted against Spain. Spain's brutal crackdown was angrily denounced in the American press, and, as a result, on February 15, 1898, the U.S. Navy battleship USS *Maine* was blown up in the Havana harbor, allegedly by Spanish agents. The American public demanded that the United States go to war with Spain to avenge the deaths of the 260 men killed in the sinking of the *Maine* and to free the Cubans from oppressive Spanish rule. The U.S. Navy blockaded Cuba and attacked the Spanish fleet in the Philippines. On May 1, **Admiral George Dewey's** fleet sailed into Manila Bay and destroyed every Spanish warship present with no American losses. On July 3, the U.S.

Navy's North Atlantic Squadron, under **Admiral William T. Samson**, demolished the entire Spanish fleet in Cuba, again with no losses. At the same time, the U.S. Army was sent to invade Cuba. Included in those forces was the **First Volunteer Cavalry** (the "Rough Riders") led by **Theodore Roosevelt (1858–1919)**, who would later serve as president of the United States (1901–1909). On July 17, the Spanish forces were defeated.

The **Spanish-American War** lasted only 114 days and cost the Americans only a handful of casualties, but the results of this victory were considerable. The Spanish subsequently surrendered not only Cuba and the Philippines but also Puerto Rico and Guam. With this victory, the United States became a world political power.

The development of an empire did little to alter American economic fortunes. Unlike its smaller European counterparts, the United States already possessed vast resources within its own boundaries. The Spanish-American War forced the United States to begin to define its role on the world stage. Because of the war and the advancing speed of international communications, a nation as inherently important as the United States could not afford to remain isolated, and it would not.

The sinking of the USS *Maine* led to the outbreak of the Spanish-American War

IN A time when women's rights were still a novelty, **Victoria (1819–1901)** was the most powerful monarch of the nineteenth century, presiding over the greatest empire the world had ever seen. Born of a German mother and a father who died when she was eight months old, she enjoyed the second longest reign—sixty-four years—of any monarch in British history. Victoria also gave her name to the era that was the golden age of British political, cultural, and industrial achievement.

Victoria was the daughter of Edward, Duke of Kent, the fourth son of George III, and Princess Victoria Maria Louisa, daughter of Duke Franz of the German duchy of Saxe-Coburg-Gotha, and sister of Belgian King Leopold I. She led a secluded life until she was eighteen years old when her uncle, **King William IV (1765–1837)**, died in 1837, and suddenly, she was **queen of Great Britain and Ireland**. The protected teenager accepted the news with cool reserve, and at her first meeting of the **Privy Council**, the **Duke of Wellington** recalled, "she not merely filled the chair, she filled the room."

Victoria married her cousin, **Prince Albert of Saxe-Coburg (1819–1861)**, on February 10, 1840, and they had nine children. After Albert's death, Victoria spent the next four decades mourning him and looking after the empire that she ruled.

As the first female British monarch in over two centuries, Victoria was a powerful presence on the throne and was destined to take an active role in affairs of state. She ruled firmly and actively, and she ruled so completely that she wouldn't allow her son, the future **King Edward VII**, to rule in her place. Even though he was almost sixty years old when she died, she remained practically active until the day of her death. Victoria was a confirmed supporter of the increasing

Queen Victoria

scope of the British Empire, which grew to the apogee of its power during the latter part of her rule and included most of Africa, as well as Canada and Australia. In 1876, her favorite prime minister, the Conservative **Benjamin Disraeli (1804–1881)**, had Parliament confer upon her the additional title of **Empress of India**. It was said, and indeed, it was true, that during Victoria's reign the sun never set on the British Empire.

The Industrial Revolution and the vast wealth derived from the empire combined to make England the cultural and technological hub of the world. London was the largest and most prosperous city on earth, and science and literature flourished there as nowhere else. The Victorian era was Britain's golden age, and it was still at its peak when Victoria died in 1901 at the age of eighty-one.

JUST AS the nineteenth century had been marked by the Industrial Revolution, the twentieth century would witness a *technological revolution*. This revolution affected all aspects of everyday life. In the field of transportation technology, the airplane would be to people of the twentieth century what the steam locomotive had been to the people of the nineteenth century. Since ancient times, many have yearned to fly like a bird, and over the centuries, legends and stories arose about people who had actually achieved this mystical, magical dream. In the fifteenth century, Leonardo da Vinci designed a nearly practical flying machine, and at the end of the eighteenth century, the Montgolfier brothers in France built the first lighter-than-air balloon that was capable of carrying people aloft. Still, the dream of human flight in a controlled, heavier-than-air vehicle remained elusive. (A heavier-than-air vehicle implies one that is held aloft by its aerodynamic properties rather than by a bag of gas.)

Several attempts at building such a machine were undertaken without success in the late nineteenth century. One failed attempt by Samuel Pierpont Langley and the Smithsonian Institution was abandoned literally days before the first successful heavier-than-air flight. This event occurred on December 17, 1903, on the sand dunes of Kill Devil Hill near **Kitty Hawk Peninsula**, North Carolina. Two men from Ohio, **Wilbur Wright (1867–1912)** and his brother, **Orville Wright (1871–1948)**, shared an interest in aeronautics from their youth and built their first unmanned glider in 1896.

The Wright brothers testing their flying machine in Kitty Hawk, North Carolina

Between 1900 and 1902 they tested a series of manned gliders at Kitty Hawk. They recognized that the key to successful powered flight would be the degree of control that the pilot could exercise over his craft. They regarded their project as an aircraft rather than as a modified kite or a machine that could be controlled in the air as a boat is in the water. The first **Wright Flyer** was a fabric-covered biplane with a wooden frame. It was driven by the Wrights' 12 hp water-cooled engine, which was connected to two contra-rotating propellers by means of belts. Wilbur and Orville completed their Flyer during the summer of 1903 and took it to windswept Kitty Hawk in December. On the 13th, Wilbur took the first turn and succeeded only in nosing the Flyer into a dune. On December 17, however, Orville Wright took to the air for twelve seconds, covering 120 feet in the first powered flight of a manned heavier-than-air craft in history. By the end of the day, each of the brothers had made two successful flights, with Wilbur covering 852 feet in his last turn at the controls.

Starting on May 13, 1904, their **Flyer 2** made a number of successful flights over the next seven months. Like the original Flyer, it manifested a tendency to stall during turns, and the Wrights went back to the drawing board. The result was the larger **Flyer 3**, which proved to be a much more reliable airplane. It was able to fly successfully over a distance of thirty-four miles. On October 5, 1905, it set an endurance record of thirty-eight minutes aloft.

UNDER THE leadership of **Emperor Meiji (1852–1912)**, who assumed power in 1867, Japan was transformed from a closed society, where its citizens were forbidden to have contact with foreigners, to a nation that was anxious to have contact with, and to emulate, the outside world. In less than half a century, Japan progressed from medieval feudalism to a modern, industrial power.

Meiji's efforts at modernization were initially met with resistance from some of the country's **shoguns** (feudal lords), but the majority of the people in positions of power could see that the advantages of opening the country to foreign trade far outweighed the disadvantages. Prior to Meiji's rule, the shoguns had commanded private armies, but in 1873, the emperor established a national army equipped with up-to-date weapons based on those of the Germans. A navy, unnecessary while Japan was still an isolated kingdom, was also created. Scholars made thorough studies of European constitutions and governmental systems, and in 1890 the **Diet**, a parliament modeled after the English system, was established.

By this time, the Japanese had come full circle from being totally isolated to becoming eager to assert themselves as a world power. From Europe, Japan emulated elements of government, military organization, and the Industrial Revolution. Next, Japan copied the concept of building an empire that extended beyond its own borders. For a country whose foreign policy had always

Soldiers fighting in the Russo-Japanese War

been to *not* have a foreign policy, asserting itself throughout Asia represented a bold, new step. Japan annexed the neighboring **Ryukyu Islands** in the 1870s, and in 1894 Japan engaged China in the **Sino-Japanese War** for control of Korea and Manchuria. At this time, China's landmass, population, and resources greatly exceeded those of Japan. However, China was under the rule of the ineffective Manchu dynasty, which served as little more than figureheads for regional warlords. China was an Asian superpower only because of its size and geographical location, and it proved itself ill-equipped for a major war. When Japan won the war in 1894, it thus succeeded in gaining a foothold on the Asian mainland.

Only the influence of the vast Russian Empire stood in the way of Japan's total domination of Manchuria and Korea. In February 1904, Japan attacked Russian ships and bases in the Far East. The **Russo-Japanese War**, the twentieth century's first major conflict, resulted in an embarrassing defeat for the Russians. For the first time since Genghis Khan, an Asian force had resoundingly defeated a major European power in a sustained series of battles. After the peace treaty was signed on September 5, 1905, Japan controlled all of northeast Asia, becoming the first world power to emerge in Asia in modern times. This victory also established Japan as a major force to be reckoned with, both politically and militarily, in the world community.

PEOPLE ONCE believed that the world was flat and that it was the center of the universe. Although the first theories to question these beliefs were treated as heresy, for several centuries we have known that the earth is neither flat, spherical, nor the center of our own solar system. Until the early twentieth century, people assumed that time was absolute, that a properly wound clock ran at the same speed everywhere, and that light always traveled in a straight line.

These assumptions were overturned by a shy, German-born physicist named **Albert Einstein (1879–1955)**, who is generally recognized as being the greatest scientific mind since **Isaac Newton (1642–1727)**. Indeed, his **theory of special relativity**, published in its basic form in 1905, is so complex that it is still not fully understood by most people. Einstein demonstrated that time was relative to the speed at which the observer is traveling. He also theorized that the speed light travels—which we understand as 186,000 miles per second—is not absolute.

Albert Einstein

The essence of Einstein's theory of general relativity is that if matter is converted into energy, then the energy released can be shown in the simple formula $E = mc^2$, where "c" represents the velocity of light and "m" the mass. The formula indicates that a small mass can be converted into a huge amount of energy. It shows mathematically a means of developing nuclear weapons and reactors for the production of nuclear energy.

Einstein's discoveries about nuclear energy also explained the nature of stars (including our own sun) by demonstrating that if the sun was really on fire, it would have been consumed years ago. In a nuclear reaction, Einstein suggested that huge quantities of light and heat could go on being created with minimal loss of mass. Although his theory is extremely complicated, one of the best explanations of relativity, in easily understood terms, came from Einstein himself when he wrote that "by an application of the Theory of Relativity to the taste of the reader, today in Germany I am called a German man of science; in England I am represented as a Swiss Jew. If I come to be regarded as a *bete noire,* the description will be reversed and I shall become a Swiss Jew for the Germans, a German for the English."

IN THE summer of 1914, Europe was a restless place. There was tension in the air. Although the continent had not seen a total war for ninety-nine years since the defeat of Napoleon at Waterloo, there had been numerous smaller conflicts, including the Franco-Prussian War of 1870, which found German forces marching into Paris. However, the massive conflicts that had marked the decades before and during Napoleon's reign remained a distant memory.

In 1815, the leading European powers, attending the **Congress of Vienna**, adopted the idea that there should be no one superpower, and that the major nations of Europe should maintain more or less equal powers. Even though this agreement generally served to produce a peaceful environment, tensions continued to boil beneath the surface. Meanwhile, the great powers of Europe had melded themselves into two alliances, which, in themselves, constituted superpowers: Britain, France, and Russia established the **Triple Entente**, while Austria-Hungary (a dual monarchy), Germany, and Italy formed the **Triple Alliance**, which also included Turkey as a de facto member. After the alliances were formally in place, there was an arms buildup, and various nations began looking to resolve their tensions with their neighbors through war. Every country had its own agenda. The French wanted the Alsace back from Germany, and Germany wanted to challenge the British fleet with its own. On a continent that was fraught with political tensions, all that was needed was one spark to set things off. Austria-Hungary, an uneasy empire in the heart of Europe, was a crucible of numerous conflicting European ethnic groups. The flashpoint that finally ignited the inevitable war occurred in the Balkan states, an area of southern Europe that would later become Yugoslavia.

When Bosnia and Herzegovina was incorporated into the Austro-Hungarian Empire, neighboring Serbia became angered because Serbians were a persecuted ethnic minority in Bosnia and Herzegovina. This annexation served to deny them direct access to the Adriatic Sea. Similar tensions erupted into war again in 1992.

Although the emperor of Austria-Hungary was eighty-four-year-old **Franz Josef I (1830–1916)**, the actual power behind the throne was his son and heir **Archduke Franz Ferdinand (1863–1914)**. On June 23, 1914, the archduke and his wife made a state visit to Sarajevo, the restless capital of Bosnia and Herzegovina, to show the flag and assert their imperial power. They were assassinated by Bosnian Serbs.

Serbia was ultimately implicated in the plot, and Austria-Hungary declared war on July 28 after a month of diplomatic haggling. Following this, the other major European nations fell like dominoes into the abyss of war. Austria had threatened Serbia, so Russia, which supported Serbia, threatened Austria. Germany, allied with Austria, issued counterthreats to Russia. France, which sought to regain territory it had lost to Germany in 1870, backed Russia. Britain, which recognized that Germany's aspirations for expansion in Europe were in conflict with its own, aligned itself with France and Russia but did not make a commitment.

Germany, believing that Britain would remain neutral and hoping for a quick victory, declared war on France on August 2. Russia, in turn, declared war on Austria-Hungary, and Britain declared war on Germany in support of its ally. Because these powers were also empires with colonies around the globe, the conflict was not confined to continental Europe. It was to become the first true *world* war, and it consumed millions of lives.

SPARKED BY the assassination of Archduke Franz Ferdinand, **World War I** officially began with a round of declarations that culminated with Britain's declaration of war against Germany on August 4. Despite having to face Russia to the east and France to the west, Germany was by far the best prepared of the nations in the conflict, and its commanders were confident of an easy victory if they acted swiftly. This led to Germany's violation of Belgium's neutrality by attacking France across the level plains of Flanders (in Belgium's northern province). Britain's close ties with Belgium (their monarchs were cousins), made this act the catalyst that catapulted Britain into the war.

French soldiers fighting from a ditch

All the major European powers subsequently embarked on what was destined to become history's most terrible war with almost a sense of verve and excitement. Those enamored of the flourish of flags and uniforms parading in the summer sunshine failed to take into account the deadly impact of a new generation of weapons, from machine guns to poison gas. Used for the first time in a major conflict, they made the new war a dreadful and decidedly unchivalrous affair.

The countries Britain, France, Russia, and Belgium faced off against Germany and Austria-Hungary while Italy, which was technically allied with the latter, reacted to public opinion at home and entered the war against Austria in order to win back control of the Italian-speaking sections of Austria.

Germany's strategic plan called for a rapid defeat of France, such as had been the case in 1870, followed by an attack on Russia, which was the least prepared of the European powers for war. Germany devoured Belgium in two short weeks and drove westward into France, executing a battle plan designed by **Field Marshal Alfred von Schlieffen (1833–1913)**, which called for a great swinging movement with the left flank anchored at Metz and the right flank extending through Belgium to Paris. The plan required a concentration of forces on the right, but **General Helmuth von Moltke (1848–1916)**, charged with implementing the scheme, failed to do so. Although von Schlieffen's plan succeeded initially, and the right flank arrived in Paris before becoming overextended, the offensive stumbled. When the French and British counterattacked along the **Marne River** on September 6–12, they were able to stop the German advance, which never again regained its momentum.

The British and French contained the Germans, but lacked enough power to push them back. Thus, what might have been a swift German victory of less than sixty days turned into a bloody stalemate that lasted four years.

AT THE beginning of the twentieth century, the Russian Empire was the largest contiguous empire in the world. However, it was also a backward, primitive place barely touched by the Industrial Revolution or the social improvements that had affected Europe during the previous century. Ruled by the thoroughly autocratic **Romanov dynasty**, it was inhabited by an increasingly restless population.

Vladimir Ulyanov, better known as Nikolai Lenin

There had been an uprising in 1905 after Russia lost the **Russo-Japanese War**, but **Tsar Nicholas II (1868–1918)** had successfully suppressed it. In 1914, Nicholas again went to war, this time against Germany. After his armies suffered defeat on the battlefield, the domestic situation began to unravel. With food supplies growing scarcer, anger toward the aristocracy, which had always enjoyed a lavish lifestyle at everyone else's expense, increased.

After numerous food riots in 1915 and 1916, a full-scale revolution erupted in 1917, and on March 2, Nicholas was forced to abdicate. Several failed attempts to establish a new government followed. However, the entire social and economic structure of the Russian Empire finally collapsed under its own weight and the strain of World War I. As anarchy and starvation swept the countryside, Russia became fertile ground for the doctrine of socialism, preached by a German academic and would-be philosopher named **Karl Marx (1818–1883)**, who believed that the masses could have plenty by simply seizing the property of the rich aristocracy. The most violent of the socialist groups were the **Bolsheviks**, who were also the most organized. They had vehemently opposed the tsar. When a government was set up by the Constitutional Democrats led by **Alexander Kerensky (1881–1970)**, they attacked him as well. On November 7, 1917, Kerensky was toppled in a bloody coup, and he lost the power to govern Russia, which led to the establishment of the **Council of People's Commissars**. The head of this council, the first premier of post-Imperial Russia, was **Vladimir Ilich Ulyanov (1870–1924)**, known by the name of **Nikolai Lenin**, who had been living in Switzerland when the revolution broke out.

Lenin's new government encountered a great deal of opposition, but in March 1918, he signed a peace treaty with the Germans and was able to bring home troops loyal to his cause to silence those who disagreed with him. On July 17, 1918, Lenin ordered the deposed tsar executed and set about consolidating his power. He united all of the late tsar's colonies into a new empire, calling them **"Soviet Socialist Republics."**

On December 30, 1922, he formed the **Union of Soviet Socialist Republics (USSR)**, a one-party state based on the ideas of Karl Marx in which Lenin's **Communist Party** wielded all of the power and controlled all of the wealth and property. In the coming decades, millions of lives and vast resources would be sacrificed in a vain effort to justify a cruel social experiment that would take seventy years to expire.

THE FIRST World War had been an exercise in futility. Entered into almost lightly, it turned into a bloody carnage that went beyond anyone's worst nightmares. Lasting four years, it consumed the lives of over nine million soldiers and ten million civilians, and it left another twenty-one million wounded. Moreover, the ground war deteriorated into a frustrating deadlock in which the major battlefronts

The signing of the Treaty of Versailles

hardly moved during the entire course of the conflict. This was because the German offensive opened the war on the Western Front, which stalled within weeks. The British and French held the Germans but were unable to push them back. The initial German victories on the Eastern Front also bogged down. When the Russian tsar was overthrown in 1917, it was logical to assume that the Germans would shift manpower from east to west and change the balance of power, but by that time, too many Germans had been killed and the Allies in France had become too well entrenched for the Germans to tip the scales.

After the British ocean liner *Lusitania* was sunk by a German U-boat, the United States declared war against Germany on April 6, 1917. After the Yanks reached the battlefield in force in 1918, the tide finally turned. The general effect of the war had been to inflict a form of national exhaustion upon the combatant nations. Millions had been killed, and at home, food and material shortages had caused widespread suffering and unrest. Russia had experienced a major revolution, and during 1918, riots and

strikes were common in both Austria-Hungary and Germany.

With the entry of the Americans into the war, the Allies were at last able to assume the offensive. The German and Austro-Hungarian will to carry on fighting crumbled in the face of mounting casualties, and by early November, both nations had agreed to accept the Allied terms for surrender. On November 9, Germany's **Kaiser Wilhelm II (1859–1941)** abdicated and fled to Holland, and on November 11, at "the eleventh hour of the eleventh day of the eleventh month," the war was declared over.

A peace conference was convened at the old imperial palace of Versailles near Paris to decide the future of Europe. Both Austria-Hungary and Germany were compelled to hand over vast stocks of weapons and supplies and to abandon large tracts of territory. In addition, Germany was forced to accept Allied occupation west of the Rhine River. The Austro-Hungarian Empire was broken into its two parts, and pieces were sliced off to form a new Serbian-dominated country called Yugoslavia. Germany, which was seen as having inflicted the most suffering, received the harshest conditions under the terms of the **Treaty of Versailles**.

The reparations that were demanded crippled the German economy such that it could not recover from the horrors of the war. Against this backdrop, the seeds of Nazi tyranny were sown. In fact, the treaty was so severe that it was in itself the basic cause of the next world war.

RADIO WAVES were discovered in Germany by **Heinrich Hertz (1857–1894)** in 1887, and this had paved the way for **Guglielmo Marconi (1874–1937)** to send the first wireless telegraph communication in 1895. However, radio as we know it today—involving actual sounds rather than just dots and dashes, as in telegraph communication—was not possible without the invention of the microphone and the **Audion**. The microphone is a device that converts complex sounds into complex electrical impulses much like the telephone patented by **Alexander Graham Bell (1847–1927)** in 1876. Invented in 1907 by American scientist **Lee de Forest (1873–1961)**, the Audion was an electronic tube that made it possible to transmit those complex electrical impulses.

Lee de Forest's Audion

Today, we take it for granted that we can turn on a small device in our homes, our offices, our cars, or even attached to our belts and hear words spoken by someone many miles away. We also take for granted the ability to switch on a box and instantaneously see moving pictures of events happening halfway around the world. Until well into the twentieth century, both of these technologies—radio and **television**—were unthinkable. Today, life without them is unthinkable.

With all the elements of the new technology available, de Forest sought to demonstrate the potential of radio by arranging for a January 13, 1910, broadcast of Enrico Caruso singing *Cavalleria Rusticana* from the Metropolitan Opera House in New York City. The first regularly scheduled radio programming did not go on the air for another decade, when Westinghouse broadcast the November 2, 1920, presidential election results from Pittsburgh, Pennsylvania.

In 1922, the British Broadcasting Corporation (BBC) was formed and broadcast its first news program on November 14. Although there were numerous early experiments with devices for converting images to electricity, it was the Scottish engineer **John Logie Baird (1886–1946)** who built the first practical television in 1923. In 1926, he demonstrated his **Televisor**, which was used for the first public television broadcast in the United Kingdom. In 1927, the Bell Telephone Company in the United States broadcast television images from Washington to New York via telephone lines, which was the first use of television in the United States. In 1928, Baird conducted the first transatlantic television broadcast from London to New York. The BBC began broadcasting regular television programming in 1930 when Baird's improved Televisor went on the market. Although Baird's invention was not an immediate commercial success, by 1939 there were twenty thousand television viewers in the United Kingdom. A French television transmitter was installed atop the Eiffel Tower in 1935, and RCA—Radio Corporation of America—installed one atop New York's Empire State Building in 1936. Because of World War II, television did not become a common fixture in private homes until the late 1940s and early 1950s.

John Baird built the first **color television** system in 1928, and Bell Labs devised a parallel system in the United States in 1929. While color television had always been theoretically possible, it did not become a commercial practicality until the late 1960s, by which time radio and television touched nearly every aspect of people's daily lives throughout most of the world.

ALEXANDER FLEMING (1881–1955) was a bacteriologist who volunteered for duty in the British Army's medical corps in 1914. During that time, he was horrified by the sight of so many men painfully enduring deep wounds crawling with bacteria, and he was unable to eradicate the germs without harming the wounded men. The antiseptics and antibiotics that existed killed bacteria, but they also destroyed human tissue as well. Because of this, they were useful only on surface wounds, and in wartime, there were many wounds more severe than surface ones.

After the war, Fleming returned to his laboratory, having decided to devote himself to the quest for a more effective antibiotic. He theorized that the answer lay in fighting the invading organisms not with a caustic chemical that also harmed the patient but with an organic substance. He believed that substances or secretions found in the human body held the key.

By 1921, this line of inquiry led him to lysozyme, a secretion from human tears, which proved successful against some bacteria but not against the most dangerous ones, such as *staphylococcus, streptococcus,* and *gonococcus.* Fleming continued his experiments with various organic substances, which he tested in small glass petri dishes in his laboratory. Occasionally, these dishes would become infected with mold spores and bacteria that naturally exist in the air, and he'd clean out the dishes and start over.

One day in 1928, he noticed that in one dish containing *staphylococci* the bacteria had been attacked by a particular mold. He began studying this mold and discovered that it dissolved nearly every bacteria with which it came in contact. This mold, *penicillium notatum,* led to **penicillin**, the

Alexander Fleming

heretofore elusive antibiotic. Penicillin had a tendency to degenerate within a few hours of being isolated from the mold, and Fleming spent the next decade exploring ways to overcome this so that the serum could be mass-produced. When World War II began, a massive effort was launched in both England and the United States to develop a durable penicillin that could be used in large quantities. In 1943, the United States Northern Regional Research Laboratory in Peoria, Illinois, isolated *penicillium chrysogenum* from a moldy melon and solved the perplexing problem. Within a year, penicillin was saving thousands of lives on battlefields and around the world.

By 1945, it was available on the civilian market, having completely revolutionized the treatment of disease. In that same year, Sir Alexander Fleming and two of his colleagues were awarded the Nobel Prize in medicine.

THE NATURE of global economic trends is predictably cyclical, economic booms that alternate with recessions. However, no recession in modern times ever plunged deeper, lasted longer, or affected so much of the world as the one that began with the crash of the **New York Stock Market** on October 29, 1929, a day known as **Black Tuesday**.

The 1920s had been an era of great economic expansion worldwide, especially in the United States. Until the twentieth century, the American economy had been largely

Americans waiting outside a soup kitchen

independent of Europe. After World War I, the United States was allied with European powers as never before, and the demand for American goods—notably, farm products—greatly increased in Europe.

As a result, the United States became the world leader in manufacturing and finance as well as in agriculture. The value of company stocks on the American stock market increased rapidly as both individuals and institutions made investments as never before. Unemployment became almost non-existent; everyone seemed to have plenty of money. In order to sell even more stocks, brokerage firms made it possible for prospective buyers to purchase stocks "on margin" by paying only a small part of the cost of shares and "borrowing" the rest against the value of the stock. While this practice seems highly questionable today with the benefit of 20/20 hindsight, the value of the stocks only went up at that time and increased so fast they were quickly worth double or triple

the purchase price. Soon the American economy turned into a vast, credit-inflated bubble.

Meanwhile, in Europe, farmers, recovered from the war, had begun harvesting crops once again, and the demand for American commodities plummeted even as American farms became more efficient and started increasing their output.

The economic bubble finally burst on October 29, 1929, when stocks across the board began to tumble in value. Because there was so much credit and so little equity and real money, personal and corporate fortunes vanished in the space of twenty-four hours. On Wall Street, many financiers who found themselves suddenly penniless jumped to their death from skyscrapers. The ripple that started on Wall Street soon became a massive wave that engulfed the nation, and finally the world. Banks failed, farm prices collapsed, businesses and factories closed, and foreign trade evaporated.

The economic crash that began in October 1929 did not hit bottom for three years. Eventually, thirty million people lost their jobs, half of them in the United States. **The Great Depression** continued for over ten years and deeply affected the lives and outlook of an entire generation. The Depression and the governmental measures taken to overcome it created a turning point in the history of twentieth-century economic policy.

HERBERT CLARK HOOVER (1874–1964) was elected president of the United States in 1928 at the height of postwar prosperity, but a year later he was faced with **Black Tuesday**, the worst worldwide economic calamity of the twentieth century. Hoover believed that governmental intervention would make matters worse and that the economy would improve on its own. It didn't. **The Great Depression** had begun.

By 1932, when Hoover was running for reelection, the value of the stock market was only 10 percent of what it had been when he was elected four years earlier. Millions of people remained unemployed, waiting desperately for the government to take constructive action. Hoover's opponent, New York's governor, **Franklin Delano Roosevelt (1882–1945)**, proposed nothing less than the most "activist" government in American history, telling people that they "had nothing to fear but fear itself."

Elected by a landslide, Roosevelt took office in March 1933 and was successful in pushing his bold, new economic plan he called the **New Deal** through Congress in just one hundred days. The Legislature gave Roosevelt an unprecedented $3.3 billion to spend on the creation of new jobs and passed the **National Industrial Recovery Act (NIRA)**, which gave the president the power to control the economy. Roosevelt hoped that the NIRA would spur private-sector economic growth, but instead it came under heavy criticism from business leaders. In 1936, it was ruled unconstitutional.

Undaunted, Roosevelt continued to propose numerous innovative—albeit controversial—New Deal programs. He proposed the **Tennessee Valley Authority (TVA)**, which built a series of hydroelectric dams on the Tennessee River to generate electricity and create jobs in one of the most economically

Franklin Delano Roosevelt

depressed regions of the country. The **Works Progress Administration (WPA)** put thousands of people to work on public works projects ranging from building bridges to writing travel guides. In 1935, Congress passed the landmark **Social Security Act**, a nationally enforced savings retirement plan that would prove to be one of Roosevelt's most lasting legacies.

Despite continuing controversy surrounding his programs, Franklin D. Roosevelt won reelection by another landslide in 1936 and went on to win two more presidential terms in 1940 and 1944.

Roosevelt died less than a year into his fourth term, but he served longer than any American president did before or since. He left a legacy of social and economic reform that still remains. Today, the largest segment of America's federal budget is an amalgam of Social Security and other social welfare programs, which are direct descendants of Roosevelt's New Deal policies.

THE ALLIES' stern measures imposed on Germany in the **Treaty of Versailles** created a situation of intense hardship and a mood of deep despair among the German people. **Kaiser Wilhelm II (1859–1941)** had abdicated in 1918, leaving Germany with a leadership void that was filled by a weak republic under the **Weimar Constitution of 1919**. Conditioned to being governed by a strong monarchy,

Adolf Hitler

the German people were disheartened by the seemingly ineffective **Weimar Republic**, which they saw as being imposed upon them because of their defeat in the war.

Against this backdrop, many political fringe groups emerged and began exploiting deep-seated discontent. These groups included socialists, Communists, and a group that called itself the **National Socialist German Workers' Party (NSDAP)**, or **Nazi Party**. The Nazis believed in a strong, centrally governed Germany, which would assume a position of dominance among the nations of Europe. They envisioned a role for Germany that was reminiscent of the tenth-century Holy Roman Empire of Otto I or the German Reich—Empire—constructed by Otto von Bismarck in the nineteenth century.

There were many leaders and visionaries within the ranks of the Nazi Party, but the man who eventually stepped into the limelight as the leader of the party was an intense Austrian named **Adolf Hitler (1889–1945)**. Hitler had served with the German army in World War I and afterward had settled in Munich. He became enthralled with the concept of German nationalism, colored with a doctrine of racial superiority that regarded Jews and other minority groups as inferior

beings. He had helped found the Nazi Party and was jailed in 1923 after a failed attempt by Nazis to overthrow the Bavarian state government. While incarcerated, he formulated a plan to seize power not only in Bavaria but also in all of Germany.

Gradually, the Nazis became recognized as a legitimate political party, and Hitler, who was a brilliant orator, began to garner wide support. By 1933, the Nazi Party was so powerful that **President Paul von Hindenberg (1847–1934)** was compelled to appoint Hitler as Germany's chancellor. Hitler promptly began to use his new position as a power base to oust Hindenberg and seize dictatorial control. He set about defying the conditions of the Treaty of Versailles by rearming and expanding the much-reduced German military and by reasserting German territorial interests in Europe.

One element of the Treaty of Versailles had been the demilitarization of the German Rhineland, a condition that the Germans perceived as a clear violation of their sovereignty. On March 7, 1936, Hitler blatantly defied the treaty by sending German troops into this area.

Had the French or British suppressed this treaty violation, Hitler would have had no choice but to withdraw and possibly resign because, at that time, his army was still very weak. However, because Britain and France were anxious to avoid a war, his actions went unopposed. Hitler's success in the Rhineland resulted in a complete rearmament of Germany, making them the world's leading military power, which ultimately led to World War II.

◆ **HUMANKIND'S GREATEST** war, an all-consuming conflict touching nearly every corner of the earth, was precipitated by the same kind of greed for political and economic power that had caused many previous wars. Italy had dreams of establishing a new Roman Empire; Germany coveted more *lebensraum* (living space) in central Europe for its growing population; and Japan envisioned itself as the new hub of a "Greater East Asia Co-prosperity Sphere." Together, these nations formed an alliance known as the **Rome/Berlin/Tokyo Axis**, or simply the **Axis**.

Prior to this time, Japan had annexed Manchuria in 1931 and had invaded China in 1937. Italy's dictator, **Benito Mussolini (1883–1945)**, whose goal was to become the first Roman emperor actually based in Rome in over 1500 years, had conquered Ethiopia in 1935. Meanwhile, **Adolf Hitler (1889–1945)** had set out to achieve his goal of acquiring more land, one step at a time.

In 1936, Hitler's armies occupied the German Rhineland in direct violation of the Treaty of Versailles. The lack of active opposition by Britain and France encouraged him. In March 1938, he annexed Austria, making it part of Germany, and in March 1939, his troops took control of Czechoslovakia. Although Britain and France complained loudly, in the interest of avoiding a war, they took no action.

On August 24, 1939, Germany signed a nonaggression pact with the Soviet Union, and on September 1, the German army launched a full-scale attack on Poland. At this point, Britain and France issued ultimatums because their mutual assistance treaties with Poland called for them to finally take action to halt Hitler's aggression. On September 3, Britain and France declared that a state of war had existed for two days.

The conflagration had begun.

◆ **AT THE** time Adolf Hitler invaded Poland on September 1, 1939, the German army and air force were the most well trained, best equipped, and overall superior military force in the world. Their coordinated air and ground offensive, known as *blitzkrieg* (lightning war), was the most rapid and efficient mode of military attack the world had ever seen. The use of fast-moving tanks, mobile forces, dive bombers, and paratroopers, who all worked together as one tight, well-disciplined force, stunned the world, especially the Polish defenders. Germany was able to subjugate Poland in just three weeks.

Following this, Britain and France dispatched a few bombers over Germany, but for the most part, a lull in World War II occurred on September 27. Throughout the winter, Allied and German troops sat and stared at one another across the heavily fortified Franco-German border. So little was happening that newspaper wags dubbed the situation the *"sitzkrieg."*

Suddenly, on April 9, 1940, Germany attacked. *Sitzkrieg* became *blitzkrieg* once again. German troops quickly occupied Denmark and Norway. On May 10, the Germans began a great offensive to the west that duplicated their advance on Belgium and France in 1914 at the beginning of World War I. By May 28, Luxembourg, Belgium, and the Netherlands had surrendered, and German forces were pouring into France. By June 14, Germany had seized control of Paris, having accomplished in five weeks what it had been unable to do in four years of protracted fighting in World War I.

France finally surrendered on June 22, leaving Britain to face the onslaught of Germany's *blitzkrieg* alone. Only twenty miles of English Channel separated Germany's crack troops from an army that had abandoned all of its equipment in France when 350,000 British and French troops evacuated and barely managed to escape from the Germans at Dunkirk on the French coast on June 4.

While Hitler's forces prepared for a cross-channel invasion of Britain, the English people rallied around **Prime Minister Winston Spencer Churchill (1874–1965)**, who had taken office on May 10, telling the people he had "nothing to offer but blood, toil, tears, and sweat." He defied Hitler by informing him that his troops would meet relentless opposition on the beaches, on the streets, and in every village. However, *Luftwaffe* (German Air Force) commander **Field Marshall Hermann Goering (1893–1946)** insisted that his bombers could easily subdue Britain and make the planned sea invasion a simple walkover.

In August 1940, the *Luftwaffe* began a brutal, unremitting bombing assault on Britain's ports, factories, and cities. The only thing that stood in the way of an easy victory was the courageous, but vastly outnumbered, pilots of the **Royal Air Force (RAF)**, who met the Germans like gnats attacking crows. Despite the fact that the British had fewer than one thousand fighters to face a *Luftwaffe* onslaught four times as large, the RAF was able to destroy twelve bombers for each one of their own losses. Churchill called it the RAF's "finest hour."

Although the **Battle of Britain** would drag on until the end of the year, the real turning point occurred on September 17 when Hitler made the decision to postpone the sea assault indefinitely.

This battle was the first major conflict in history to be decided solely by airpower, and it brought Hitler's remarkable string of successes to a halt. The RAF's turn back of Germany's *Luftwaffe* would later prove to be the point at which the tide of the war began to slowly turn in favor of the Allies.

◆ **THE BATTLE OF BRITAIN** was a major setback in Germany's effort toward world domination, but it did not stop Hitler's armies. Britain remained alone and isolated for a year while the rest of the countries in continental Europe either allied themselves with Germany, became occupied territories, or waited in anticipation of a German attack. The Germans successfully took control of Bulgaria, Romania, Yugoslavia, and Greece, and on June 22, 1941, Hitler launched **Operation Barbarossa**, an invasion of the Soviet Union.

During the first two years of the war, the United States remained apart from the hostilities while continuing to give moral support to Britain. Although Americans felt a close affinity with the British due to their similar cultures and democratic governments, they were anxious to remain separate from the bloodshed of "Europe's War." However, **President Franklin Delano Roosevelt (1882–1945)** was well aware of the probability that the United States would eventually be drawn into the war. As they had in World War I, German submarines begun attacking American ships in the Atlantic. Roosevelt met secretly with British prime minister **Winston Spencer Churchill (1874–1965)** in August 1941, and the two leaders agreed to work together if the United States was forced into the war.

Meanwhile in Asia, Japan, Germany's Axis ally, continued to expand the empire that it called the Greater East Asia Co-prosperity Sphere by invading Indochina and the Netherlands East Indies. Roosevelt, increasingly concerned about Japanese aggression, ended exports to the island nation and considered further sanctions. Japan viewed these actions as a major impediment to their plans to dominate the Far East and decided to take action. Germany's offensive against Russia seemed to enjoy great success, and Britain was virtually surrounded. From the Japanese perspective, the only obstacle in the way of a worldwide Axis victory was the U.S. Navy's presence in the Pacific Ocean. Thus, Japan planned to execute a single, bold masterstroke to eradicate this threat.

At 7:30 on Sunday morning, December 7, 1941, bombers launched from Japanese aircraft carriers struck at American military installations in Hawaii, particularly the **Pearl Harbor Naval Base**. The attack was a complete surprise and an immense success. When it ended, three thousand Americans were dead, one hundred aircraft were destroyed, and the U.S. Navy's Pacific Fleet was decimated. Eight battleships that had been anchored in Pearl Harbor had been put out of commission.

The following day, President Roosevelt, calling December 7 "a day of infamy," asked Congress for a declaration of war. On December 11, Germany and Italy declared war against the United States, and Japan declared war on Britain. Though this was certainly one of the darkest moments in World War II, with American resources committed to the war effort, it would be only a matter of time before the Axis was toppled.

The United States joined the war after the attack on Pearl Harbor Naval Base

IN THE months following the attack on Pearl Harbor, the military successes achieved by the Japanese were reminiscent of the German *blitzkrieg* of 1939 and 1940. Within a month of Pearl Harbor, they had captured Wake Island, Guam, Hong Kong, and the allegedly impregnable British fortress at Singapore. After landing in the Philippines, they seized control of the capital at Manila and cornered a doomed garrison of Americans on the Bataan peninsula. The Japanese Empire now encompassed most of the Pacific, including three of Alaska's Aleutian Islands and nearly all of the Asian mainland's coastline from Korea almost to India, and plans were being made to invade Australia.

At the same time, Hitler dominated all of continental Europe. His armies had reached the gates of Moscow in December 1941, but a combination of the Russian winter and the armed resistance of the Russian military forced a retreat. However, in the spring of 1942, the Germans counterattacked, successfully regaining much of what they had lost. The Axis now controlled most of North Africa from the Atlantic almost to the Nile River and were poised to assault Cairo and the Suez Canal. In the summer of 1942, the Allies, seriously worried about losing the war, knew that before the tide could be turned in their favor, they would have to stop the relentless momentum of the Axis war machine. In the Pacific, the crucial

US aircraft in the Battle of Midway

turning point occurred as a Japanese invasion fleet sailed toward Midway, an island at the head of the Hawaiian archipelago. On June 3, 1942, they met the U.S. Navy in a fierce four-day battle, which mainly took place between carrier-based aircraft. When the **Battle of Midway** was over, the U.S. Navy had lost one carrier, but the Japanese had lost four, two of them heavy cruisers. Forced to retreat, the Japanese momentum was crushed, and they were never again able to mount a major offensive.

In North Africa, the German drive toward the Suez Canal was blunted on July 1, 1942, by the British at an obscure Egyptian town called **El Alamein**. Although the German *Afrika Korps* survived, from that point onward, the Axis forces in North Africa were forced into total retreat.

On the German Eastern Front with Russia, where more soldiers on both sides died than on all other fronts combined, the tide finally turned when the Russians steadfastly refused to surrender the city of **Stalingrad** (now Volgagrad) to the German invaders. The **Battle of Stalingrad**, considered one of the most costly of the war, raged throughout the bitter winter of 1942–1943, with the Germans finally surrendering on February 2, 1943.

After these defeats, although the Axis still possessed great strength, their strategic position worldwide shifted from the offensive to the defensive.

ALTHOUGH THE momentum of World War II had shifted in 1943, it was not until 1944 that the Allies were able to amass sufficient numbers of troops and equipment to finally crush the Axis. After winning the **Battle of Stalingrad**, the Soviet army, known as the Red Army, began an aggressive offensive drive. After successfully forcing the Germans out of Russia in 1944, the Red Army pushed them back through Poland and Romania, engaging in some of the largest land battles in world history.

At the same time, American and British bombers undertook a wide-ranging strategic bombing offensive aimed at destroying the German railroad network and industrial infrastructure. During 1943, the Allies succeeded in driving the Germans from North Africa, recaptured Sicily, and landed in Italy. After Italy surrendered, the Germans were compelled to redirect troops to the homeland in order to prevent an Allied invasion.

In the Pacific, 1943 was a year of holding actions, but in 1944, the Allies, under the command of **General Douglas MacArthur (1880–1964)**, launched a series of major offensives aimed at retaking Japanese-held islands. Guam and the Mariana Islands were recaptured in August, providing bases for Boeing B-29 Superfortress bombers to strike at the Japanese mainland. On October 20, MacArthur landed in the Philippines to begin a two-month campaign of liberation.

The largest military operation of 1944—and indeed of the entire war—was the Allied **invasion of Normandy** in northern France on June 6. Under the leadership of **General Dwight David Eisenhower (1890–1969)**, 2.9 million Allied troops, 5,000 ships, and over 15,000 aircraft took part in crossing the English Channel from England to land on the Normandy coast. The landings

U.S. soldiers in northern France

were a success, and by August 25, the Allies marched triumphantly into Paris.

By the end of 1944, Germany and Japan had lost control of most of what they had conquered. Although they had no hope of winning World War II, they continued to desperately fight, making the final Allied victory a very costly one for all sides.

THE ANGLO-AMERICAN Allies brought the war home to Germany early in 1945, reaching the banks of the Rhine River by March 8. Russia's Red Army swept through Hungary and Austria and began closing in on Berlin from the east. On April 19, Russian and American forces met at the Elbe River, and Berlin was surrounded. Adolf Hitler committed suicide in his fortified bunker on April 30, and on May 7, which was designated **Victory in Europe (VE) Day**, Germany formally accepted Allied terms for unconditional surrender.

US service members on VE day

With the defeat of Germany, the Allies turned their attention to conquering the Japanese Empire. The Japanese had become more and more tenacious in their defense of the Pacific islands as American forces moved closer to Japan. With this in mind, the Allies estimated that it would cost them a million casualties—most of them American—to recapture the islands. **Harry S. Truman (1884–1972)**, who became president upon the death of Franklin D. Roosevelt on April 12, 1945, decided that such a prospect was unacceptable. By this time, the United States was in the final stages of developing nuclear weapons (then known as atomic bombs). Truman, along with his cabinet and top military advisers, decided to use two of the new bombs against Japan with the hope that such a maneuver would cause the Japanese to surrender immediately, thus saving a costly military campaign.

On August 6 and August 9, American Boeing B-29 Superfortress bombers detonated atomic bombs over Japan, first at **Hiroshima** and then at the southern city of **Nagasaki**. The bombs each had the explosive power of fifty thousand tons of TNT, and they had the desired effect. On August 14, Japan sent word that it would accept Allied conditions for an unconditional surrender.

The formal surrender was signed on September 3, 1945, which was officially designated as **Victory over Japan (VJ) Day**. The signing took place aboard the U.S. Navy battleship USS *Missouri* amid a vast armada of Allied ships in Tokyo Bay.

The world's bloodiest war was over at last, but in the wake of a hard-won peace, there lurked the ominous specter of the terrible destructive power of nuclear weapons. The reality of such weapons would significantly affect the outlook of all future generations.

Casualties of World War II

	Military Deaths	Total Deaths (Civilian and Military)
United States	416,800	418,500
United Kingdom	383,600	450,700
Soviet Union	8,800,000–10,700,000	24,000,000
China	3–4,000,000	20,000,000
Germany	5,533,000	6,600,000–8,800,000
Italy	301,400	457,000
Japan	2,120,000	2,600,000–3,100,000

STALIN'S IRON CURTAIN

1946

THE TERM "Iron Curtain," coined on March 5, 1946, by Britain's wartime prime minister **Winston Spencer Churchill (1874–1965)** during a speech in Fulton, Missouri, came into common usage immediately after World War II. It described the new political reality that had descended upon Europe in the wake of the war: a reality that would shape global politics for the next forty-five years.

From the precipice of defeat in 1941, the Soviet Union's leader, **Joseph Stalin (1878–1953)**, had rallied his people, built the world's largest army, and helped vanquish Germany in 1945. In the process of liberating numerous sovereign states from German possession, Stalin's enormous Red Army had occupied all of the previously independent states that lay between Poland and Romania. Stalin then announced that he had no intention of withdrawing his forces from these territories, using the pretext that he wanted to maintain a buffer zone between Germany and the Soviet Union so that Germany would never again be able to accomplish what it had in 1941.

Britain and the United States, the Soviet Union's wartime allies, decried Stalin's total domination of Eastern Europe, but they had, in fact, helped to make it a reality. In February 1945, as World War II neared its end, Stalin, Churchill, and **President Franklin Delano Roosevelt (1882–1945)** met at Yalta in the Soviet Crimea to discuss the configuration of postwar Europe. Stalin expressed his interest in permanently crippling Germany and maintaining "friendly" states in Eastern Europe. Although Roosevelt and Churchill didn't like this idea, Stalin promised to allow some form of democracy in the countries placed under his control, and the Western leaders, anxious to believe him, agreed to his plan. Roosevelt also did not oppose Stalin because he wanted to maintain the "Grand Alliance" of these three powerful nations after the war, believing that such an alliance would best preserve world peace. Churchill didn't oppose Stalin's new empire because he feared that if he objected, Stalin would insist that Great Britain dismember its own empire.

Roosevelt died two months after the Yalta Conference. Within a year, Stalin withdrew the USSR from the Grand Alliance. Less than a decade later, the British Empire was all but gone.

Stalin was, in fact, a ruthless dictator who, during the 1930s, had directed so many "purges" of known or suspected opponents in his own country that he had actually killed more of his own people than the Germans did during the war. Like his nemesis, Adolf Hitler, Stalin was a charismatic man who ruled with an iron fist with no use for democracy or elections and who tolerated no views contrary to his own. Although Stalin was a communist, his motivation sprang not so much from a desire to perpetuate the doctrines of that economic philosophy but rather from his political concept of a powerful Soviet Union surrounded by nations that were totally under its control. To this end, he supported a communist revolution in China that ultimately succeeded in 1949 and numerous other attempted power grabs around the globe. He had contemplated using the Red Army to swallow Western Europe but was held in check by the American nuclear arsenal and the implicit threat that an attack on Western Europe would invite American nuclear retaliation.

Even after Stalin developed nuclear weapons in 1949, this threat remained. Thus began the **Cold War**, a forty-five-year-long nuclear stalemate between the United States and the USSR, two nations that came to be known as superpowers.

THE ERA of the **Ming dynasty (1368–1644)** was the golden age of Chinese culture. During this time, the city of Peking (now known as Beijing) was built and the arts flourished. This dynasty was succeeded by the **Ch'ing (Manchu) dynasty (1644–1912)**, and ethnic Manchurians ruled China. The Manchu dynasty began with a period of political expansionism that eventually turned into the opposite—the domination of China by foreign powers.

Mao Tse-tung

During the nineteenth century, China lost a series of minor wars with several European powers, and eventually "leases" were imposed, which led to several Chinese port cities becoming virtual colonies of foreign nations. Germany took Tsingtao; Portugal claimed Macao; France annexed Kwangchow; Russia took possession of Dairen; and Britain declared Kowloon and Hong Kong British colonies.

When the Ch'ing dynasty collapsed in 1912, the **Kuomintang (Nationalist) Party** declared a republic, and **Dr. Sun Yat-sen (1866–1925)** became president. The new Chinese Republic took advantage of World War I to purge most of the foreign enclaves in the country, but unfortunately, they were simply replaced by others ruled by Chinese warlords, making it impossible for the Kuomintang to unite China as a single entity.

Sun's successor, **General Chiang Kai-shek (1887–1975)**, faced opposition not only from the warlords but also from a major Japanese invasion that began on July 7, 1937. The Japanese had seen themselves as more powerful than China since the Sino-Japanese War of 1894. So in one sense, the 1937 invasion was simply another chapter in the same quest for total domination of the Far East. Chiang soon lost much of Kuomintang-controlled China to the Japanese. When the Allies declared war against Japan in 1941, Chiang's Nationalist China allied itself with them. Although the Allies never actually drove the invading forces out of China, the Japanese withdrew as part of their unconditional surrender signed on **VJ Day**.

During the war, Chiang had nominally allied himself with the Chinese communist leader **Mao Tse-tung (Mao Zedong) (1893–1976)**. After the Japanese withdrawal, Mao initiated a civil war for control of the country. Mao had built a solid power base among the peasantry, who had suffered through years of war and foreign domination, and his movement steadily gained ground.

On October 1, 1949, Chiang's Kuomintang government fled to the island of **Taiwan**, and Mao declared his country to be the **People's Republic of China**. The entire Chinese mainland was now united under ethnic Chinese rule for the first time since 1644. The Communists imposed a stern and rigid societal structure that would not loosen until reformers took over after Mao's death in 1976.

IN THE years immediately after World War II, the power of the atom that had ended the war was hailed as the energy source that would revolutionize and enrich the lives of people around the globe. It was also predicted that nuclear energy would be cost-effective and plentiful. The first power-generating nuclear reactor started operating in the United States in 1951, and soon after, **President Dwight D. Eisenhower (1890–1969)** announced his **Atoms for Peace** plan, through which the U.S. government would finance reactors around the world and furnish technical help to provide this inexhaustible energy source for everyone.

The theory of nuclear energy was first advanced by the renowned physicist **Albert Einstein (1879–1955)** in his **theory of relativity** (1905), in which he stated that energy was equal to mass at the speed of light ($E = mc^2$). In other words, mass could be converted into energy if it were propelled at the speed of light. The first **nuclear reactor**, or device built to contain a self-sustaining nuclear chain reaction, was constructed at the University of Chicago. Built under the direction of Italian physicist **Enrico Fermi (1901–1954)**, who had won the 1938 Nobel Prize in physics, the world's first controlled nuclear chain reaction took place on December 2, 1942. The U.S. Army underwrote the construction of this reactor as a first step toward the **"Manhattan Project"**—the development of a nuclear weapon that was ultimately used to win World War II.

In 1945, attention turned to what appeared to be a promising source of low-cost electrical energy for civilian use. In theory, nuclear energy is simple: a nuclear reaction creates intense heat that can be used to produce steam, which turns turbines to produce electricity. The world's first power-generating nuclear reactor was the **Experimental Breeder Reactor (EBR)**, designed at the American Argonne National Laboratory, which began producing electricity on December 20, 1951.

Small nuclear reactors were later adapted for use aboard ships, particularly submarines, because they offered a limitless range without the necessity of refueling. The first such vessel was the U.S. Navy's submarine USS *Nautilus,* which was launched on January 21, 1954. The first nuclear-powered merchant ship was the *Savannah,* launched in 1959, and the first nuclear aircraft carrier was the USS *Enterprise,* armed in 1960. The same year, the nuclear submarine USS *Triton* was the first vessel to travel around the world underwater without refueling.

The **Atomic Age** was heralded with much excitement and optimism, but by the early 1970s, serious questions began to arise about the safety of nuclear reactors. Their cores are highly radioactive, and hence, there is a potential danger of catastrophically contaminating the areas around them if there is a mishap. This fear was confirmed on March 28, 1979, when an accident at the **Three Mile Island** nuclear power plant in Pennsylvania released giant clouds of radioactive steam. The worst nuclear accident in history occurred on April 28, 1986, when the **Chernobyl** nuclear power plant, in what is now Ukraine, exploded, rendering much of the surrounding countryside uninhabitable and killing thousands of people.

After these accidents underscored the dark side of the Atomic Age, the use of nuclear energy fell into disfavor, particularly in the United States, where construction of new nuclear power plants came to a standstill. Elsewhere, most notably in France, Germany, and Japan, a new generation of hopefully safer plants began operation in the early 1990s.

EVEN BEFORE humans had mastered the ability to fly in the air in heavier-than-air machines (see no. 63), science fiction writers, such as Jules Verne, inspired and intrigued the public with stories of human beings flying not just in the immediate atmosphere but into outer space.

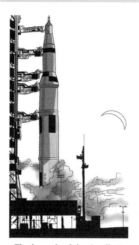

The launch of the Apollo 8

Until the middle of the twentieth century, most people assumed that it was highly improbable that anyone would ever actually travel in space because the practical problems of escaping earth's gravity and supporting human life in outer space seemed insurmountable. However, the tremendous technological advances that occurred during World War II changed everything. The most notable development during this era was the **V-2 rocket**, which was designed in Germany by **Dr. Wernher von Braun (1912–1977)**. After Germany's defeat, V-2 technology was captured both by the United States and the Soviet Union and used as the basis of independent rocket programs in both countries. In 1957, the Soviet Union succeeded in launching **Sputnik 1**, the first object made on earth and placed in orbit around the earth. This was the vital first step in achieving the dream of seeing human beings in outer space.

The launch of Sputnik 1 also initiated a politically inspired "space race" between the United States and the Soviet Union, with the obvious goal of being the first nation to launch one of its own citizens into orbit. Over the next four years, both countries launched unmanned spacecraft, including some that were specifically in preparation for manned missions.

Finally, on April 12, 1961, the Soviet Union launched **Vostok 1**, which was piloted by **Yuri A. Gagarin (1934–1968)**. He became the first human in space and completed one orbit of the earth before returning to a hero's welcome. The first American in space, **Alan B. Shepard (1923–1998)**, made his flight only three weeks later, on May 5. By the end of 1961, two Soviet **cosmonauts** and two American **astronauts** had flown in space, but the Americans did not actually orbit the earth. The first American to orbit the earth was **John Glenn (1921–2016)**, on February 20, 1962.

Within the first five years after Gagarin's flight, the Soviets conducted eight manned space flights, and the Americans flew twelve in their **Mercury** and **Gemini** spacecraft. The first woman in space was Soviet cosmonaut **Valentina Tereshkova (b. 1937)**, who was launched for forty-eight orbits aboard Vostok 6 on June 16, 1963.

Having achieved the dream—and the engineering feat—of human space flight, both the United States and the Soviet Union turned their attention to other goals in space exploration. In December 1968, the United States' **Apollo 8**, carrying Frank Borman, James Lovell, and William Anders, became the first manned space flight to leave earth's orbit and fly into deep space. The Apollo 8 ventured farther from earth than people ever had before. They traveled a quarter of a million miles and placed their spacecraft into orbit around the moon. Within a year, their fellow astronauts would reach the moon's surface.

◆ **JOHN FITZGERALD KENNEDY (1917–1963)** took office as president of the United States in 1961, promising a vigorous new America. However, the most serious crisis that his administration would face sprang from the festering **Cold War** between the United States and the Soviet Union that dated from the end of World War II.

An uneasy stalemate had prevailed for over fifteen years when **Premier Nikita Khrushchev (1894–1971)** decided to take advantage of Kennedy's preoccupation with his domestic agenda to consolidate the Soviet position around the world. The first manifestation of this occurred on August 13, 1961, when Soviet and East German troops suddenly began constructing a concrete wall nearly two stories high through the center of Berlin, emphasizing the postwar partition of Germany and effectively closing the border between the East and West. The **Berlin Wall** was a profound manifestation of the political realities of the Cold War. It became a symbol of Western political failure and of the Soviet Union's virtually unlimited power, and it proved to be a deep embarrassment for Kennedy.

Another major source of difficulty was the Caribbean nation of Cuba, where the Soviet-backed communist leader **Fidel Castro (1927–2016)** seized power in 1959. In April 1961, shortly after Kennedy assumed office, a U.S.-sponsored invasion at Cuba's **Bay of Pigs** failed, which made the United States appear inept while angering both the Soviets and the Cubans. In September 1962, Khrushchev announced to Kennedy that any further attacks on Cuba would be considered an act of war. Soon after, it was discovered that the USSR had been positioning medium-range missiles, equipped with nuclear warheads, in Cuba. These missiles, which could strike major American cities

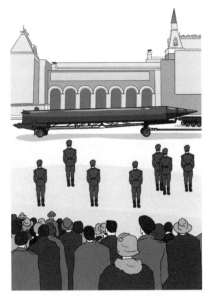

A Soviet medium-range missile in Moscow during the Cold War

within a short time, represented a direct threat to the security of the United States.

On October 22, Kennedy went public and demanded that the USSR withdraw the missiles or the United States would attack Cuba. Thus began the week during the Cold War known as the **Cuban Missile Crisis**, which would draw the two superpowers extraordinarily close to an all-out nuclear holocaust. The results of such a mutual retaliation would have devastated at least half of the major population centers of both nations.

A flurry of negotiations ensued as both sides prepared for war. American warships surrounded Cuba to enforce a "quarantine" on all shipping, and American bombers moved into position in Florida in readiness for an air assault. Finally, on October 28, Khrushchev told Kennedy that he would remove all missiles if the United States would promise not to invade Cuba.

It was the hottest moment of the Cold War, but World War III had been averted.

◆ **OF ALL** the political assassinations in the twentieth century, only that of Archduke Franz Ferdinand in 1914—an event that precipitated World War I—had more far-reaching effects than the murder of America's thirty-fifth president on November 22, 1963. **John Fitzgerald Kennedy (1917–1963)** traveled to Texas to make a series of political appearances. The 1964 presidential election was less than a year away, and his popularity in the South had suffered because of his strong support for civil rights legislation.

On November 22, Kennedy was sitting in an open car in a motorcade winding its way through the city of Dallas when shots rang out. One bullet pierced his neck, another destroyed half his skull, and yet another wounded Texas governor **John B. Connally**, who was riding in the same car.

It was the first assassination of a major world leader since the advent of television and instantaneous global communications. Broadcasts of the events surrounding the assassination, including Kennedy's funeral two days later and the killing of **Lee Harvey Oswald (1939–1963)**, the alleged assassin, by **Jack Ruby (1911–1967)** on live television, captured the attention of the world.

In the United States, where the boyish, vigorous Kennedy, noted for his gifted oratory, had fired the imagination of the postwar generation, there was a profound sense of shock and grief. For many who came of age during the 1960s, Kennedy's death would prove to be a seminal occurrence in their lives. For many Americans, the loss of their president was compounded by the fact that Kennedy's youth and charisma did not live on in his successor, **Lyndon Baines Johnson (1908–1973)**. Johnson is most well remembered for escalating the nation's involvement in the Vietnam War, the most unpopular war in American history, and for introducing the **Great Society**, a series of federally funded programs designed to tackle persistent social problems such as poverty, which many believe was well-intentioned but poorly executed.

Because Oswald was murdered only two days after Kennedy, he was never tried and convicted. In order to end widespread speculation of a conspiracy, President Johnson ordered a special commission, headed by Supreme Court **Chief Justice Earl Warren (1891–1974)**, to investigate the assassination. The **Warren Commission** investigation was seen by its critics as more of an indictment of Lee Harvey Oswald than an objective study of all available evidence, and this became an important element in the erosion of the American people's confidence in their government that occurred in the ensuing decades. Indeed, when the U.S. Congress reopened the investigation in 1978, it was concluded that a second gunman in another location had fired at Kennedy and, in fact, had probably fired the fatal shot. However, the identity of the second gunman was never ascertained, and no irrefutable evidence has yet surfaced to support any of the many conspiracy theories that have proliferated over the years.

The most profound impact of Kennedy's assassination was on the outlook of the American people, which changed from one of hope and optimism to one of cynicism. After World War II, the United States emerged as the world's economic superpower, and over the next two decades it enjoyed the greatest prosperity of any nation in the history of the world. President John F. Kennedy's death brought the nation face to face with its own vulnerability.

THE ANCESTORS of most African Americans arrived in North America as slaves taken against their will from their homes in Africa, and most slaves worked in the American South. In the North, there was a strong **abolitionist movement**, which sought to abolish slavery throughout the United States. When the abolitionists succeeded in gaining substantial influence in the federal government, the South seceded from the Union in 1861.

Dr. Martin Luther King Jr.

President Abraham Lincoln (1809–1865) fought the Civil War to preserve the Union, and in 1862, he took the first legal step toward eradicating a root cause of the war by issuing the **Emancipation Proclamation**, which eliminated slavery in all states—both North and South—effective January 1, 1863. After the Civil War, the rights of former slaves were guaranteed by the **Thirteenth Amendment** to the Constitution (1865), which encoded Lincoln's Emancipation Proclamation into constitutional law; the **Fourteenth Amendment** (1868), which made former slaves citizens of the states in which they resided; and the **Fifteenth Amendment** (1870), which gave *male* former slaves the right to vote. (It would take fifty years more for American women of any color to gain the right to vote.)

Despite these amendments, many Southern states continued to maintain local laws, which curtailed the rights of Black Americans. In a practice known as **segregation**, certain public facilities, from drinking fountains to seats on city buses, were restricted to "whites only." Private businesses, such as restaurants, had the right to exclude Blacks from their establishments. Even public schools remained segregated until 1964.

In the 1950s, a movement to end segregation began in many places throughout the South. This movement sought to assert the civil rights of Black people to integrate themselves into the rest of society and to fully guarantee that they could exercise their legal rights, such as the right to vote. In 1955, **Reverend Martin Luther King Jr. (1929–1968)**, a charismatic Black minister, emerged as a major leader of the **Civil Rights Movement** when he organized a boycott of the segregated bus system in Montgomery, Alabama.

Over the next nine years, the Civil Rights Movement gained both momentum and support, especially after **John F. Kennedy (1917–1963)** became president in 1961. The climax of the movement was a massive civil rights march on Washington, DC, in the summer of 1963 that culminated with Dr. King's immortal "I Have a Dream" speech on August 28.

On July 2, 1964, the **Civil Rights Law** was enacted, which outlawed all forms of discrimination in public facilities, accommodations, and schools. That same year, Dr. King was awarded the **Nobel Peace Prize** for his work in promoting the civil rights of African Americans. Even though Dr. King was assassinated in 1968 (see no. 89), the quest for equal civil rights for all peoples continues to this day.

THE VIETNAM WAR (1964–1975) was a major turning point in American, and world, history, and the **Tet Offensive** of 1968 was the pivotal event of that war. Following World War II, the United States was assured of its role as a superpower. At the same time, it saw itself as a world leader charged with the responsibility to maintain order and a balance of power in the world. Part of that role was also perceived to be a mandate to stop the tide of **Communism** from drowning the smaller nations around the globe.

This included Southeast Asia, where South Vietnam and Laos were fighting a guerrilla war against communist insurgents (known as the **Viet Cong** and **Pathet Lao**, respectively), who were receiving support from communist North Vietnam. In the mid-1960s, President **Lyndon Baines Johnson (1908–1973)** decided that a show of American military might would serve to intimidate North Vietnam. When American warships were attacked by North Vietnamese patrol boats in the **Gulf of Tonkin** on August 2, 1964, Johnson ordered American warplanes to counterattack North Vietnam. He also greatly increased the number of American military advisers in South Vietnam. Within a year, the number of American troops had grown to more than 180,000, and they had become actively involved in combat.

Over the next three years, the number of American soldiers in Vietnam surpassed 500,000, and the death toll mounted. Despite this enormous investment in personnel and money, nothing seemed to change. The Viet Cong controlled about as much territory in South Vietnam in 1967 as they had in 1964. The war seemed to have reached a stalemate. However, the Johnson administration continued to insist that the war was all but won, and they had the statistics to prove it, which fueled talk of a "**credibility gap**" by those who believed Johnson was lying. Although the younger generation—those under twenty-five—were becoming increasingly angry and disillusioned with America's involvement in Vietnam, their parents, who had lived through World War II still gave Johnson the benefit of the doubt.

On the ground in Vietnam, the period around the **Lunar New Year (Tet)** was typically a period of lessened military action. However, on January 31, 1968, in the midst of Tet, the North Vietnamese and the Viet Cong launched a massive offensive throughout South Vietnam. They managed to capture one wing of the American Embassy in **Saigon**, the capital of South Vietnam.

Although the United States eventually fended off the attacks, it took over a month to stem the tide. The Tet Offensive conclusively proved that after three years of American intervention in Vietnam's civil war, neither the will of the Communists had been broken nor had their ability to wage war lessened in any way.

The Tet Offensive was deeply embarrassing to Johnson—especially since it was an election year—and on March 31, he announced that not only would he not seek reelection but that he hoped to enter into peace negotiations with North Vietnam. Tet ended the political career of an American president, but it gave North Vietnam the encouragement it needed to continue a war that many had considered all but over.

After suffering the loss of more than 58,000 lives, the United States finally withdrew all its troops from South Vietnam in 1973. On April 30, 1975, North Vietnam finally defeated South Vietnam and united the country under communist rule, which continues to this day.

WITH THE exception of the years consumed by the two World Wars, there hadn't been a year marked by such deep rifts in the social fabric of the Western world since 1848. French university students went on strike in May 1968 and were joined by workers in a national strike that affected ten million people. The riots and social upheaval that had struck Paris in May were compared to that of the French Revolution of 1789. In the United States, 1968 witnessed the culmination of a turn in the course of American history that had begun with the John F. Kennedy assassination in 1963.

Public trust in government and established institutions, which had been strained by Lyndon Johnson's **credibility gap** over the true nature of the war in Vietnam, almost ceased to exist for a large portion of a generation that had been born since World War II. The **Tet Offensive** proved that Johnson had misled the American people about Vietnam and almost caused him to become the first incumbent president to lose a presidential primary, when antiwar activist **Senator Eugene McCarthy (1916–2005)** came within three hundred votes of defeating him in the March 12 New Hampshire primary.

Beginning with Johnson's withdrawal from the presidential race on March 31, the United States was jarred by an unprecedented series of blows against the social fabric of the nation:

April 4: The **Reverend Martin Luther King Jr. (1929–1968)**, the nation's foremost Black leader and an eloquent advocate of a nonviolent approach to achieving civil rights, was gunned down in Memphis, Tennessee, touching off a massive wave of riots in 125 cities.

June 5: **Senator Robert Francis Kennedy (1925–1968)**, the younger brother of John F. Kennedy and the leading candidate for the Democratic presidential nomination, was assassinated in Los Angeles moments after winning the California primary election.

August 20: Shortly before midnight, two hundred thousand Soviet and Warsaw Pact troops invaded Czechoslovakia to depose the nation's progressive leader, **Alexander Dubček (1921–1992)**, who had begun to dismantle communist totalitarianism in his country. This demonstrated that the repressive doctrine of Joseph Stalin (see no. 81) was still alive and well. The United States, embroiled in Vietnam and wracked by nationwide civil unrest, was unable to come to Czechoslovakia's aid.

August 26: As events were unfolding in Czechoslovakia, the Democratic National Convention convened in Chicago amid massive antiwar demonstrations and rioting. Numerous people were injured by what was later described as an overzealous police force, and even the candidates found themselves breathing tear gas. The presidential nomination, which probably would have gone to Robert Kennedy had he lived, was won by **Vice President Hubert Humphrey (1911–1978)**.

November 1: As the Vietnam War continued to work against Humphrey's candidacy, Lyndon Johnson grounded American warplanes in Vietnam in a desperate attempt to help Humphrey capture the votes of those opposed to the war, and thus win the election.

November 5: Hubert Humphrey lost the election to Republican candidate **Richard Milhous Nixon (1913–1994)**. He won with only 43 percent of the popular vote. The Third Party candidate, **George Corley Wallace (1912–1998)**, won more votes than any Third Party candidate in American history. Both factors were symptomatic of the deep discontent seething in the United States.

HAVING ACHIEVED the dream of successfully supporting human life in outer space in 1961, both the United States and the Soviet Union committed themselves to sending one of their citizens to the moon and back. Although the details of the Soviet effort remained shrouded in secrecy for nearly three decades, the American project was highly publicized.

By the mid-1960s, both nations had developed, and successfully flown, a spacecraft capable of carrying more than one crew member, a development that was essential to mastering the complexities of flying to the moon. After the Soviets beat the Americans into space with the first manned flight, the United States pulled ahead with a highly successful series of ten flights of the two-man **Gemini** spacecraft in 1965 and 1966, including a 330-hour mission, whose duration would not be matched until the early 1970s.

The design for the American lunar mission involved the **Apollo** spacecraft, which would carry a crew of three from the earth to orbit around the moon. Two members of the crew would then travel to the lunar surface, remain for several days, and then rejoin their colleague for the return trip to earth. The first manned Apollo spacecraft **(Apollo 7)** was test-flown in earth's orbit in October 1968. On December 21, 1968, **Apollo 8** became the first manned spacecraft to fly to the moon. On Christmas Eve, Frank Borman, James Lovell, and William Anders became the first humans to orbit another celestial body. No landing was planned, and Apollo 8 returned home safely.

Two further training flights followed in early 1969, and on July 16, 1969, **Apollo 11** was launched from the Kennedy Space Center in Florida, destined to take the first humans to the surface of the moon. On July 20, **Neil Armstrong** and **Edwin "Buzz"**

The crew of the Apollo 11 planted an American flag on the surface of the moon

Aldrin left **Michael Collins in** lunar orbit and descended to the surface. A few hours later, Armstrong became the first human to set foot on a celestial body other than earth.

Between November 1968 and December 1972, six more Apollo spacecraft made the three-day, quarter-million-mile journey from the earth to the moon. All except **Apollo 13**, which experienced an inflight emergency, landed two astronauts each on the lunar surface.

As Neil Armstrong had said, it was "one giant leap for mankind." It was made even greater by the fact that after those dozen men walked the dusty surface of earth's moon, no other humans would equal their accomplishment in the twentieth century.

THE CREATION of the **State of Israel** on May 14, 1948, angered the Arab world because the new Jewish state was composed of land claimed by both Arabs and Jews. Israel repelled an attack by **Arab League** countries—mainly Syria, Jordan, and Egypt—in 1948 and launched a counterattack on Egypt in 1956. However, aside from these flare-ups, a general stalemate prevailed, during which Israel continued to insist on its right to exist, a right that the Arab world refused to recognize.

On June 5, 1967, the Arabs commenced a major assault aimed at the total destruction of Israel. In what was to be called the **Six-Day War**, the Arab plan backfired when Israel not only repelled the attack but also captured Arab territory equivalent to twice the area of Israel proper, including Egypt's Sinai Peninsula, the Jordanian-controlled old city of Jerusalem, the West Bank of the Jordan River, and Syria's Golan Heights.

The oil embargo led to higher prices on petroleum products and long lines at gas stations

The embarrassed Arab nations, particularly Egypt and Syria, rearmed themselves in preparation for another siege. The second effort by Arab states to destroy Israel occurred on the Jewish Holy Day of **Yom Kippur**, October 6, 1973. This time the Arabs, especially the Egyptians, fared better. However, a massive airlift of Western aid, particularly American, bolstered the Israeli defenders, allowing them to thwart the advances of the Arab armies and to retain most of the gains they had achieved in the Six-Day War in 1967.

The Arab world, which had long accepted Western aid to Israel without overt complaint, reacted harshly, showing a level of unity that had been uncommon since before the collapse of the **Ottoman Empire**. This new Arab Union even included nations such as Saudi Arabia, which had never taken an active part in the wars against Israel, and collectively, the Arab states decided to use their vast oil resources, upon which the West depended, as an economic weapon. On October 17, 1973, they declared an embargo on all shipments of oil to Europe and North America. The impact of the embargo was felt immediately, as affected countries were forced to institute rationing and stockpiling measures. Even after the Arab oil embargo was finally lifted, on March 18, 1974, oil prices remained at more than double what they had been a year earlier.

The impact of the 1973 Arab oil embargo upon the international economy was significant, and it left a permanent, worldwide legacy. The cost of petroleum-based products, particularly plastics, doubled, and research into alternate energy sources was stepped up. Western countries realized that they could no longer depend upon an inexhaustible supply of cheap oil from the Middle East. After 1973, the industrial world was never the same.

ALTHOUGH RICHARD MILHOUS NIXON (1913–1994) was elected president of the United States in 1968 because of the failure of the Johnson/Humphrey administration to resolve the Vietnam War, Nixon continued to support the American presence in Vietnam after his election. He even went so far as to authorize an American invasion of Cambodia on April 29, 1970, which resulted in the most massive wave of antiwar demonstrations yet seen. A student protest on the campus of **Kent State University** in Ohio on May 4 resulted in the death of four students when National Guardsmen fired "warning shots" to disperse a crowd of chanting protesters.

In 1972, as Nixon faced reelection, he became involved in covert efforts to spy on, and discredit, his opposition. These efforts culminated in a burglary at the Democratic Party's headquarters in the **Watergate Building**.

At the same time, divisions within the Democratic Party resulted in the nomination of a left-of-center candidate, **Senator George McGovern (1922–2012)**, who many saw as having little support among the majority of the electorate. This, combined with Nixon's announcement on the eve of the election that "peace is at hand," resulted in his victory at the polls.

Nixon's second term in office was the most troubled of any American president. As the Watergate burglars went on trial early

Richard Nixon announcing his resignation on the radio

in 1973, there was much public speculation that some of Nixon's closest aides had been directly involved in planning the break-in. In the wake of mounting accusations that Nixon himself had been actively involved in a massive White House cover-up of the affair, the U.S. Senate convened investigative hearings. Chaired by Senator Sam Ervin, the Watergate hearings lasted from May 17 to November 15, 1973, and eventually uncovered proof that a number of White House and intelligence community personnel had been party to the Watergate break-in and subsequent cover-up. The accused included H. R. Haldeman, John Ehrlichman, John Dean, and Attorney General Richard Kleindienst, all of whom were forced to resign their positions.

At the same time, Nixon had appointed his own special prosecutor, Archibald Cox, who he subsequently fired on November 26 after Cox discovered evidence that Nixon himself was involved in the cover-up. From that point on, Nixon refused to cooperate with any further investigation. On July 24–30, 1974, the House Judiciary Committee voted three articles of impeachment against him. On August 8, Nixon announced that he would resign the presidency to avoid being removed by impeachment.

When Richard Nixon resigned in disgrace, a new era of disillusionment, cynicism, and distrust of government—politicians in particular—dawned in America.

◆ **IN THE** century following the death of **Muhammad (570–632 CE)**, Islam's founder, his followers succeeded in spreading Islamic doctrine and political influence from India to France (see no. 22). Between 1096 and 1270, Christian Europeans came to blows with Islam in the **Crusades** (see no. 26), and there were numerous wars between adherents of the two religions in the ensuing centuries. The rise of European colonial powers in the eighteenth and nineteenth centuries coincided with a waning of Islamic political power, but even though the nations of North Africa and the Middle East came under the European sphere of influence, they remained religiously Islamic.

At the end of World War II, Turkey's **Ottoman Empire**, the last vestige of the great Islamic Empire of the eighth century, collapsed. However, despite universal Islamic opposition to Israel, efforts at achieving political unity among the Arab states were not successful. In 1958, under Egyptian president **Gamel Abdel Nasser (1918–1970)**, Egypt and Syria formed the short-lived United Arab Republic, and in 1973–1974, the Arab oil-producing countries banded together under the auspices of the **Organization of Petroleum Exporting Countries (OPEC)** for an oil embargo against shipments to Europe and North America.

In the years following the oil embargo and the 1973 **Yom Kippur War**, a new force that cut across political and territorial boundaries emerged from a common root of the Arab world: Islam. By the end of the 1970s, there was a general feeling among religiously conservative Muslims that the secular governments of their nations had become too westernized. As examples, they pointed to Nasser's successor, **Anwar Sadat (1918–1981)**—who signed a peace treaty with Israel on March 26, l979—and to Iran.

In Iran, which follows Islamic doctrine but is not an Arab nation, the shah, **Mohammad Reza Pahlavi (1919–1980)**, used the wealth he acquired after the increase in oil prices in 1974 to create a modern, western style economy. However, the shah was doing so within the context of a ruthless, totalitarian police state. Because of this, he had neither the sympathy of devout Muslims nor the emerging westernized middle class. When unrest began in 1978, the shah's authority quickly crumbled, and he was forced into exile on January 16, 1979. Replaced by a succession of military and civilian leaders, the shah left civil war in his wake.

On February 11, 1979, **Ayatollah Ruhollah Khomeini (1902–1989)**, an Islamic fundamentalist who ruled Iran by strict Islamic doctrine, declared Iran an Islamic Republic. Because of his intense hatred of the United States, which had supported the shah, Khomeini ordered the seizure of the American Embassy in Iran's capital city of Tehran on November 4, 1979. Subsequently, fifty-two people captured at the embassy were held hostage for the next 444 days. This lengthy **Iran Hostage Crisis**, as it came to be known, had serious effects on the American political scene. The inability of **President Jimmy Carter (b. 1924)** to resolve the crisis was one of the major factors that led to his defeat in the 1980 presidential election to his Republican challenger, **Ronald Reagan (1911–2004)**.

The existence of an orthodox Islamic government in a large nation like Iran generated unrest throughout the Islamic world. The assassination of Egyptian president Anwar Sadat in 1981 was one repercussion. This unrest continues to affect the political landscape of North Africa and the Middle East even today.

COMPUTERS HAVE drastically changed the face of modern civilization since the 1980s. The machines once known as "electronic brains" are now capable of countless tasks that would have been unthinkable before.

In 1937, American engineer Howard Aiken designed the **IBM Mark I**, which used vacuum tubes and had electromechanical switches. The first truly **electronic computers** were developed as a result of the technological boom fostered by World War II. The first electronic computer was **Colossus I**, built in 1941 for the British government at the University of Manchester by Alan Turing and M. H. A. Neumann. It helped to crack the German's secret **Ultra Code.** Colossus was followed in 1942 by the thirty-ton **Electronic Numerical Integrator & Computer (ENIAC)**, which was developed for the U.S. government by **John Mauchly** and **John Presper Eckert** at the University of Pennsylvania. The first commercially successful electronic computer, the **Sperry Universal Automatic Computer (UNIVAC)**, was designed by Eckert and Mauchly and introduced in 1951.

The **transistorized computer**, in which sturdy transistors replaced cumbersome and fragile vacuum tubes, was designed in 1958 by **Seymour Cray** for Control Data Corporation. This started a trend toward building computers that were much smaller and faster.

Cray later formed his own company and developed a series of leading-edge supercomputers. The **Cray 1** supercomputer, introduced in 1975, was capable of one hundred million operations per second. In 1985, it was superseded by the **Cray 2**, which was capable of 1.2 billion operations per second. The Thinking Machines, Inc. **CM-200** supercomputer, which was introduced in 1991, could perform 9.03 billion operations per second.

The idea of a **personal computer** in every home was born in the Santa Clara Valley south of San Francisco, California, an area that was destined to become known to the world as **Silicon Valley**. In 1976, **Steve Jobs (1955–2011)** and **Steve Wozniak (b. 1950)** created a microprocessor computer board called **Apple I** in Jobs's parents' garage, and the two men began to manufacture and market the Apple I to local hobbyists and electronics enthusiasts. Early in 1977, Jobs and Wozniak founded **Apple Computer, Inc.**, and in April of that year, they introduced the **Apple II**, the world's first personal computer.

The microcomputer revolution exploded in the late 1970s and early 1980s as Apple shipped tens of thousands of their inexpensive computers worldwide, and the idea of a home computer became reality. Businesses and educational institutions that would never have been able to buy computers—or train people to use the complex computer languages—were now able to take advantage of this technology. Apple grew quickly and continued to dominate the industry until the giant IBM Corporation introduced its **personal computer (PC)** in August 1981.

By the 1990s, microcomputers could be found in businesses, schools, and homes around the world. Technology companies continued competing to consistently release smaller, cheaper, faster, and better models, and laptops soon became popular in the early 2000s. **Smartphones**—computers that could fit in your pocket, like the BlackBerry—soon took over, and in 2007 Apple released the first iPhone, which went on to dominate the market.

AFTER JOSEPH STALIN'S Red Army swept across Eastern Europe in 1945 and pulled down the Iron Curtain, it seemed that communist totalitarianism would forever hold that part of the world in its grip. In Hungary in 1956 and in Czechoslovakia in 1968, the Soviet government acted quickly and ruthlessly to quell any spark of rebellion. With its powerful military force and an all-pervasive secret police apparatus, there seemed little doubt as to the permanence of the Soviet Communist Empire.

The hammer and sickle is a symbol of communism

The first hint of Communism's impending demise came in 1980, when Polish workers formed a non-communist trade union. Called **Solidarity**, this union, led by a shipyard worker named **Lech Walesa (b. 1943)**, demanded higher wages and the right to strike as well as expanded political freedoms. Although efforts were made to suppress Solidarity and martial law was imposed, Solidarity survived. Soviet leader **Leonid Brezhnev (1906–1982)**, who had ordered the 1968 invasion of Czechoslovakia, threatened to do the same to Poland but never actually sent troops. In 1979, Brezhnev did send Soviet troops into neighboring Afghanistan to support a faltering communist government. Planned as a quick intervention, it, instead, lasted a decade.

When Brezhnev died in 1982, he was replaced by a succession of aging leaders who governed for only brief periods. Meanwhile, the Afghanistan incursion had deteriorated into an unwinnable war between Soviet troops and entrenched insurgents. Finally, in 1985, a much younger and more progressive leader took power. **Mikhail Gorbachev (b. 1931)** proposed a much freer, more open government. Implicit in his reasoning was a belief that the Red Army should no longer intervene in Eastern Europe to support the communist political ideology, and in 1988, Gorbachev ordered the Red Army out of Afghanistan. Once Soviet countries realized that restrictions had been eased, the communist system disintegrated with unexpected speed.

In Poland, Solidarity was legalized in 1989 and won 99 percent of the seats in the new Senate. The Polish Communist Party subsequently voted to disband itself in January 1990. In Hungary, which opened its borders in May 1989, the Communist Party renamed itself in November, but still lost in free elections held in March and April 1990. The Czechoslovakian reform movement, called the **Velvet Revolution**, began in October 1989, and led to the dissolution of the Communist Party and the election of **Vaclav Havel (1936–2011)**, a dissident playwright and poet, as president in December 1989. In August 1990, Bulgaria elected its first non-communist leader, although the party retained a role in the government until the October 1991 elections. In Romania, dictator **Nicolae Ceausescu (1918–1989)**, along with his wife, was executed in December 1989, but former Communists continued to hold power. Civil discord continued throughout 1991 until a government headed by non-communists was elected in February 1992.

Although Yugoslavia broke into its pre-World War I components and erupted in a series of bloody civil wars, the rest of the Eastern European nations were able to freely pursue their own political and economic futures for the first time in over fifty years.

AT THE end of World War II, a defeated Germany had been divided into four zones, each occupied by one of the victorious Allied powers. In 1949, Britain, France, and the United States withdrew their military governments, and their former occupation zones became the **Federal Republic of Germany**, or Bundesrepublik Deutschland (BRD). However, the Soviet Union refused to allow its eastern zone to become part of the BRD. A communist state, ruled by German communist leaders, was established under Red Army "protection" that was called the **German Democratic Republic** or Deutsch Demokratische Republik (DDR).

The border between the BRD and DDR was sealed, and the two Germanys evolved separately for forty years. The idea of reunification became a lost dream. The construction of the **Berlin Wall** through the center of the former capital in 1961 served to underscore this fact. Anyone attempting to cross the wall, or indeed any part of the border, was shot by East German border guards and left for dead.

In 1989, however, a wind of change began blowing through Eastern Europe, and it stirred the people of the DDR as well. Soon many thousands of East Germans, anxious to escape, reached the BRD by traveling through Hungary, which had opened its borders. In November 1989, people suddenly attacked the Berlin Wall, bashing it with rocks and sledgehammers. East German guards, who had earlier been ordered to kill anyone who dared to come near it, did nothing. While guards on both sides of the wall looked on in awe, thousands of people began tearing the terrible symbol apart with their bare hands.

The DDR's communist government disintegrated and its first non-communist government was elected in March 1990, with its sole agenda being reunification.

In November 1989, citizens of East and West Germany began tearing down the Berlin Wall

On July 3, 1990, an economic union took place using the BRD currency, the Deutschmark. On October 3, 1990, the DDR ceased to exist, and its six regions became states of the BRD. The first all-German elections in fifty-eight years were held in December 1990.

Although much work remained to reconcile the profound economic and social disparities between the two halves, most Germans were glad to have their nation whole once again.

FOR NEARLY seventy years, the Soviet Union stood as a monolith dedicated to the concept of a one-party state, where the Communist Party ruled the country like a stern father figure who knew what was best for his children. **Joseph Stalin (1878–1953)**, who ruled from 1924 to 1953, built a powerful international security mechanism and a huge, centrally planned economy. A man known to execute anyone who stood in his way, he helped to defeat Nazi Germany and then fashioned an empire in Eastern Europe as a buffer between the USSR and the West. His successors, **Nikita Khrushchev (1894–1971)**, who ruled from 1953 to 1964, and **Leonid Brezhnev (1906–1982)**, who ruled from 1964 to his death, inherited an authoritarian machine that concentrated power within the Communist Party and for the men who controlled the Party. Both men shared Stalin's vision of an omnipotent USSR backed by the might of the Red Army. Both suppressed internal dissent in the same way, with Khrushchev crushing the Hungarian Revolt in 1956 and Brezhnev handling the situation in Czechoslovakia in 1968.

In 1979, Brezhnev tried the same tactics in **Afghanistan**, but for the Red Army, fighting Muslim guerrillas in the Hindu Kush mountains soon deteriorated into a military stalemate reminiscent of the American experience in the jungles of Vietnam. The negative impact on domestic politics caused the established order in the USSR to begin to crack.

In 1985, three years after Brezhnev's death, a new, reform-minded leader

Mikhail Gorbachev

came to power. **Mikhail Gorbachev (b. 1931)** promised *glasnost* (openness) and *perestroika* (restructuring) of the Soviet Union. However, the communist state had already begun to crumble, and only the iron bands of totalitarianism held the pieces in place.

As Gorbachev loosened them, the fifteen republics clamored for more autonomy, and the Baltic republics of Estonia, Latvia, and Lithuania sought complete independence. **Boris Yeltsin (1931–2007)**, who was elected president of the vast Russian Republic in June 1991, demanded more autonomy for his republic, which formed the heart of the USSR.

On August 19, 1991, a group of communist hard-liners arrested Gorbachev and declared a return to a Brezhnev-style state. To their surprise, Yeltsin stood up to them, and their coup failed within a few days. Although Yeltsin had succeeded in rescuing Gorbachev, it was clear to everyone that the governing structure of the Soviet Union had completely dissolved.

Gorbachev tried for several months to keep them together, but the Soviet Communist Party and the USSR were collapsing under their own weight. On December 25, 1991, the familiar red flag emblazoned with the hammer and sickle that represented seventy-five years of Soviet Communism was lowered for the last time and replaced by fifteen flags of fifteen newly independent republics. Effective on the first day of 1992, the Soviet Union and the Soviet Communist Party officially ceased to exist.

TO SAY that the **internet** has shaped world history would be a huge understatement. In fact, it is difficult to identify a facet of day-to-day human life that has remained unaffected by our ever-growing use of and reliance on the internet. Since its inception and rise in popularity, it has completely revolutionized the way we communicate, interact, learn, work, entertain ourselves, and live our lives.

The internet as we know it today grew from research and developments dating back as far as the 1960s, when the United States Department of Defense began using **packet switching**, which was an early method of grouping and transmitting data over a digital network. In 1969, the Department of Defense established the **Advanced Research Projects Agency Network (ARPANET)**, the first wide-area packet switching network, which linked computers at certain research institutions via telephone lines. In 1981, the National Science Foundation funded the **Computer Science Network (CSNET)**, expanding access to ARPANET. By the early 1990s, many more networks had been created, and because the set of rules for how to send and receive information (the internet protocol suite) had been standardized, these networks were now able to link. On December 20, 1990, researchers at CERN, the European Organization for Nuclear Research, published the very first website on the **World Wide Web (WWW)** and made their web browser public in August 1991. This marked the beginning of web resources becoming accessible over the internet. These resources, which could include web pages, documents, and other types of media, were (and still are) identified by **Uniform Resource Locators (URLs)**, also known as web addresses.

By the late 1990s, the web was quickly becoming more widely used by people all over the world as more and more browsers and websites became available, including emailing and messaging services, forums, blogs, and online shopping websites. By 2000, the internet carried 51 percent of the information flowing through two-way telecommunication. By 2007, it was 97 percent; the rapid growth was being driven in large part by the boom of community-oriented sites like YouTube, Facebook, and Wikipedia.

The rise in popularity of smartphones like the BlackBerry and Apple iPhone in the early 2000s made the internet mobile and further encouraged the use of the internet for social purposes. The rise of video streaming services in the 2010s began to revolutionize how people accessed and consumed entertainment.

The internet is constantly growing and changing, which will undoubtedly continue to influence human society and culture for as long as we continue using it.

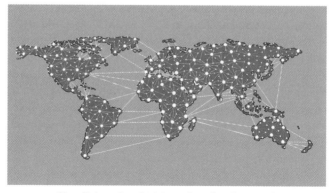

Since its invention, the internet has played a central role in shaping human history and culture

THE IDEA of a united Europe has been considered since before 800 CE, when Charlemagne first formed what would eventually become the Holy Roman Empire. Most of Europe's history has been marked by long-standing and conflicting regional interests: Imperial France, the Austro-Hungarian Empire, and

The symbol of the European Union

Prussian-dominated Germany, to name a few. Napoleon and Hitler were among those who tried to unite Europe by force. Unification without political domination seemed impossible.

By the end of World War II, virtually all of Europe had suffered destruction of its infrastructure and economic base. Although the Soviet Union and the United States set themselves up as the centerpiece of opposing military alliances, Europeans looked among themselves for economic alliances.

The first postwar economic alliance was the **Belgium/Netherlands/Luxembourg (Benelux) Alliance** of 1944–1948, followed by the Anglo-German coal and steel agreement, which became the **European Coal & Steel Community (ECSC)** in 1951, with Italy and the Benelux countries also joining. These six became the core of the **European Economic Community (EEC)**, which was established in 1957, with Denmark, Ireland, and the United Kingdom becoming members in 1973. The purpose of the EEC—also known as the **Common Market**—is to abolish internal tariffs, determine a single tariff structure for dealing with nonmembers, and allow a free movement of labor and capital among members. The EEC—now known simply as the **European Community** (EC)—was the first step toward an eventual economic unification of all of Europe.

In 1965, the EC met to form a European Parliament, which would be located in Strasbourg on the Franco-German border and serve as an economic commission that would become the basis for a future political entity. In 1979, a **European Monetary System (EMS)** was established to promote a **European Currency Unit (ECU)**.

In 1986, with Spain, Portugal, and Greece added as members, the **European Parliament** passed the **Single Europe Act**, calling for a "Europe without frontiers" by 1992. An important next step was the signing of the Maastricht Treaty on December 9, 1991, which called for the creation of the European **Economic & Monetary Union (EMU)**. As implied by its name, the EMU was to work toward a complete economic union, using ECU as a common currency for the continent by the year 1999.

By 1992, the "Europe without frontiers" envisioned for that date was largely a reality among the original members of the EC. At first, the Maastricht Treaty received only a lukewarm acceptance from the voters in other existing member nations because the traditional trappings of nationalism that had so long divided Europe were still deeply ingrained. Among the twelve existing members, borders became virtually nonexistent, and progress continued toward a monetary union. More importantly, an equal number of other nations, from the traditionally neutral Sweden and Switzerland to the new democracies of Eastern Europe, began to express an interest in becoming part of a united Europe.

ON TUESDAY, September 11, 2001, a series of four coordinated terrorist attacks were committed against the United States by the Islamist terrorist group **al-Qaeda**. Four commercial airplanes were hijacked by the terrorists, with a goal of crashing each one into an iconic American building and causing mass casualties. Two planes hit the **World Trade Center** in New York City, one hit the **Pentagon**, and the last, heading for Washington, DC, was diverted by passengers and crashed into a field in Pennsylvania. The deadliest terrorist attack in human history, the events on 9/11 caused the deaths of 2,977 victims, injured over 25,000 others, and triggered a new normal of heightened security and anxiety; anti-terrorism legislation all over the world; and a decades-long military campaign.

On September 20, 2001, **President George W. Bush** announced to Congress his intention to target and end extremist terrorism, saying, "Our war on terror begins with al-Qaeda, but it does not end there. It will not end until every terrorist group of global reach has been found, stopped, and defeated." Soon after these comments, Operation Enduring Freedom began, with the United States launching airstrikes in Afghanistan targeting al-Qaeda and the **Taliban** (the Islamist political group in control of Afghanistan's government). Within the next few months, the United States, Britain, Turkey, Italy, Germany, the Netherlands, France, and Poland all announced they would deploy troops to Afghanistan. The United States took over Kandahar and Kabul, former Taliban strongholds, by the end of 2001. Taliban forces regrouped in neighboring Pakistan and launched insurgent-style attacks against the United States, its allies, and the new Afghan government in late 2002.

By 2011, large parts of Afghanistan had been retaken by the Taliban, and nearly 140,000 foreign troops operated in the country, but on May 2 of that year, U.S. Navy SEALS in Pakistan located and killed **Osama bin Laden**, a founder of al-Qaeda and the mastermind of the September 11 (9/11) attacks. U.S. forces remained in Afghanistan for another decade, signing a peace deal with the Taliban in February 2020 and agreeing to pull troops out if the Taliban agreed not to allow its members or other groups to threaten the security of the United States or its allies again. As the United States was finishing withdrawing their troops in the summer of 2021, the Taliban launched a major offensive in which they captured most of Afghanistan, including Kabul, on August 15, 2021, driving out the democratic government and reestablishing Taliban rule in the country. By the end of August, the last American military plane left the country, leaving Afghanistan without U.S. military presence for the first time in twenty years.

In addition to Afghanistan, the 9/11 attacks and subsequent War on Terror also led to military offensives in the Philippines, Iraq, Northern Africa, and Yemen, resulting in more than 10,000 American casualties by 2021. It triggered countries around the world to strengthen their anti-terrorism laws, and led the United States to create a new agency called the **Department of Homeland Security** in 2002. The **Transportation Security Administration** (TSA) was also created, and airport security in the United States (and soon around the world) was dramatically increased. It also led to the controversial **PATRIOT Act** in the United States, which gave the government and law enforcement significantly more power to conduct surveillance and detain individuals suspected of involvement in terrorism. It irrevocably ushered in a new era of increased anxiety and heightened global security.

TRIVIA QUESTIONS

TEST YOUR knowledge and challenge your friends with the following questions. The answers are on the pages listed.

1. Octavian declared war on Egypt and defeated the armies of his triumvirate colleague, Mark Antony, in a decisive engagement in 31 BCE. Name the battle, and name Mark Antony's wife, whose armies were also involved (see no. 18).

2. In what year was Jesus Christ believed to have been born (see no. 19)?

3. Also known as China's "First Emperor," he began work on the Great Wall in about 200 BCE, introduced centralized government, and standardized numerous aspects of life. Name him (see no. 15).

4. In 261 BCE, his armies crushed the Kalingas in a particularly brutal war. After witnessing the horror of battle, he converted to Buddhism and renounced military conquest as a national policy. Domestically, he established institutions to serve the welfare of the people he governed. Who was this "enlightened" monarch (see no. 14)?

5. After signing a sixty-three-part document granting civil rights to his subjects, he said, "I will never grant such liberties as will make *me* a slave." Name the monarch and the agreement that he reluctantly signed (see no. 27).

6. In 3100 BCE, he created the world's first empire by unifying Upper and Lower Egypt. Who was this Egyptian pharaoh (see no. 4)?

7. Before his twenty-fourth birthday, he had invented calculus and discovered the spectrum of light. In 1667, at the age of twenty-five, he was elected a fellow at Trinity College in Cambridge, England, where he developed his **Three Laws of Motion**. In his work, known as the *Principia,* he demonstrated the structure of the universe, explained the movement of the planets, and calculated the mass of the Sun, the planets, and their moons. Name him (see no. 37).

8. Although they were undertaken for other purposes, the real historic importance of these military campaigns was the fact that it brought Europe in contact with the East. Many believe that these events were the catalyst that led to the **Renaissance**. What are these campaigns known as (see no. 26)?

9. Arrange the following events in chronological order from the earliest to the most recent: a) Waterloo; b) The Plague; c) The Renaissance; d) Sir Isaac Newton's discoveries; e) The French Revolution; f) The Magna Carta.

10. In approximately 440 BCE, in the period known as "The Golden Age of Greece," a philosopher with the gift of wit developed a large following. He forwarded ideals such as wise men governing for the general good and defining people's roles with one another and their environment. He was Plato's teacher. Name this brilliant philosopher (see no. 11).

11. At the start of the American Civil War, the North outmanned the South three to one and had nine times the industrial capacity of the South. Despite these advantages, the first major clash between

North and South was an overwhelming victory for the South. Name the battle and the year it happened (see no. 53).

12. In the year 1789, this Austrian-born monarch remarked, "Let them eat cake," when told that her subjects had no bread to eat. So out of touch with the average citizen, her husband, the king of France, declared the nobility exempt from taxes. The king, queen, and their family were eventually arrested and executed. Name the king and his queen (see no. 43).

13. On December 2, 1942, this event took place at the University of Chicago. What was this milestone event, and name the person under whose direction it occurred (see no. 83).

14. Soon after the Civil War, the Constitution of the United States underwent three significant amendments: the Thirteenth Amendment in 1865; the Fourteenth Amendment in 1868; and the Fifteenth Amendment in 1870. Explain the meaning of each of these three amendments (see no. 87).

15. In 1271, two brothers from the Italian city-state of Venice returned to China, taking along the teenage son of one of the brothers. Kublai Khan, the Mongol emperor of China, made the teenager an ambassador at large, sending him on missions within China, Burma, and Tibet. Name this pioneer who expanded Europe's horizons (see no. 29).

16. He defied conditions of a treaty by rearming and expanding his country's military. Due to the weakness of his army, at that time, it is believed that had the French or British suppressed his blatant treaty violation, this leader would have been forced to withdraw his troops and possibly resign. Who was this German leader (see no. 74)?

17. In about 1200 BCE, these people took to the sea and became the world's first major maritime trading power. They colonized lands from Cyprus to Corsica to Spain, and in 810 BCE, they founded Carthage. Who were these people (see no. 7)?

18. Legend has it that these two brothers were thrown into the Tiber River. Remarkably, they survived and were nursed by a she-wolf. The brothers founded a new city on Palatine Hill. Name the two brothers and the city (named after one of the brothers) (see no. 8).

19. At the end of the Second Punic War, Hannibal met his match in an effort to protect the city of Carthage. On October 19, 202 BCE, Hannibal's string of successes came to an end in a decisive battle with the armies of this Roman general. Name the battle and the Roman general (see no. 16).

20. After this eighth-century leader consolidated the states of northern Italy under Frank control, he found that his long-range strategies were compatible with those of Pope Adrian I. With the spiritual and political blessing of the pope, he went on to expand his empire (which included France and most of Italy) by adding much of Denmark, Germany, and central Europe, as well as Spain. Name this "Emperor of the Romans," who was actually French (see no. 23).

PROJECT SUGGESTIONS

1. Four of the most famous demagogues in history, Alexander the Great, Napoleon Bonaparte, Adolf Hitler, and Joseph Stalin, ruled empires centered upon Greece, France, Germany, and Russia. However, these men were not Greek, French, German, and Russian, although these nations were at the heart of their empires. Their actual nationalities were Macedonian, Corsican (his parents were Italian), Austrian, and Georgian. In each case, their empire included their own homeland. Research this interesting phenomenon and discuss reasons why it happened that foreigners came to be the absolute rulers of these countries. Can you find other cases where this happened? Can you imagine how it might happen in your country?

2. Research and compare the civil and legal codes written under Hammurabi and Napoleon or those set out in the English Magna Carta and the U.S. Constitution. How are they similar and how are they different? How did the earlier ones affect the later ones?

INDEX

OUT NOW: